TASK-CENTERED CASEWORK

TASK-CENTERED CASEWORK

WILLIAM J. REID

AND

LAURA EPSTEIN

COLUMBIA UNIVERSITY PRESS

NEW YORK AND LONDON · 1972

ACKNOWLEDGMENTS

THE AUTHORS owe much to many people who have contributed to the development of the system of casework presented in this book. We are particularly indebted to two of our colleagues at the School of Social Service Administration, the University of Chicago: Rae Meltzer, who generously contributed her time and clinical expertness to the planning and supervision of the major field test of the service model, and Emanuel Hallowitz who, in his capacity as Director of the Social Service Department, the University of Chicago Hospitals and Clinics, made it possible for this test to be carried out. We are especially grateful to the students and professional practitioners who conscientiously used the model as a guide—as far as it could take them—in trial cases. Mary Everett, Larry Hagen and Kathleen Sullivan of the Department of Psychiatry not only tried out our approach with a number of clients but also provided us with continuous and perceptive feedback on the progress of these trials through a series of case conferences.

We needed to obtain systematic data in order to make use of these field tests in the development of the model. Joan Kwiatkowski, a doctoral student at the School of Social Service Administration, not only helped us collect the necessary data but assisted ably in all phases of data processing and analysis.

We have discussed our work with several thousand practitioners and students in courses, conferences, institutes and workshops. Many of the ideas in this book have their origins in these dialogues, which we hope proved as stimulating to our audiences as they did to us.

We have tried to give appropriate credit in the text to authors whose work has shaped our own endeavors. But citations are not able to convey the extent of our indebtedness to some of our colleagues whose writings and informal communications have so influenced us over the years that we are unable to say where their ideas leave off and ours begin. Among this group we include Helen Perlman of our faculty; Florence Hollis, Columbia University; Howard J. Parad, University of Southern California; and Ann W. Shyne, Child Welfare League of America.

We are grateful to the critics who reviewed the book before it went to press: Helen Perlman, John Schuerman, and Audrey Smith of our faculty, and Albert Schrekinger, University of Kansas. Their thoughtful and perceptive comments led to significant revisions in the final manuscript.

Finally, we were fortunate to have the services of two secretaries who type with their brains as well as their fingers: Virginia Lehman, who worked on preliminary drafts of the book, and Esther G. Silverman, who took time away from her duties as research specialist, to prepare the final manuscript.

CONTENTS

TASK-CENTERED CASEWORK

CHAPTER ONE

OBJECTIVES AND FRAMEWORK

TASK-CENTERED casework is a system of time-limited treatment for problems of living. Since this system makes use of much that is familiar in casework practice, some readers will not see it as remarkably innovative. But since we call for these familiar methods to be used within a rather novel structure, others will view task-centered casework as a decided departure from classic principles.

Where our system of treatment may fall on a traditional-radical scale has not been a matter of great concern to us. We have been rather concerned with developing an approach that will prove useful to practitioners, teachers, and students of casework. To this end we have drawn on a range of theories and practices. We have been guided by the findings of research, when such were available or obtainable, and by our clinical experience, when empirical evidence was lacking. Our labors have brought forth a system that is, by design, eclectic, incomplete, and open to infusions from other points of view and to modifications indicated by subsequent research.

The system can be better evaluated through its practice applications than by the labels that we or others may attach to it. We hope that the testing we have begun (and will report in this book) will be carried forward by agencies and practitioners who see merit in our work.

OBJECTIVES

While this book is essentially about task-centered casework, it was written to satisfy several goals. Our initial purpose, and one that has remained important, was to contribute to the systematization of brief, time-limited casework. There is need for a more detailed and comprehensive statement of the assumptions, goals, strategies, and techniques that characterize this form of practice. For the most part the theoretical literature on planned, brief casework consists of sketchy descriptions of short-term methods used in agency projects or is confined to the limited perspectives of crisis theory. This conceptual lag has been largely due to the pragmatic origins of much short-term practice. Shortages of professional staff, waiting lists, pressures on agencies to serve larger numbers of clients, disillusionment with results of long-term treatment, and empirical evidence suggesting that briefer, less costly approaches may do as well, have combined to push agencies and practitioners into greater use of planned, short-term treatment.

As often happens when a method is used because of its practical advantages, the formulations that should logically undergird and shape practice have not been adequately developed. As a result much short-term practice is carried out under theories devised for more traditional, long-term forms of treatment. One frequent consequence is a lack of fit between treatment strategy and structure. The practitioner may attempt somehow to compress a year or two of treatment into a few weeks or may simply offer a kind of lopped-off version of open-ended treatment. Thus it is not uncommon to find short-term cases with planned durations of six to twelve interviews that begin with a protracted period of exploration to garner information never to be utilized and that take on ambitious goals never to be achieved. Another consequence is perhaps even worse: short-term practice may be grossly devalued since its results tend to be measured against accomplishments *expected* of extended treatment. By this standard short-term treatment becomes a second-best alternative, whose use must be justified on grounds of expediency, even though it may actually *achieve* as much as long-term treatment.

In sum, short-term casework is badly in need of a theory of its own. Much of this book is devoted to meeting this need. Although we present a particular system of treatment, most of our formulations are relevant to the practice of brief, time-limited casework in general. Our notions concerning specification of the target problem and treatment goals, establishing the treatment contract and maintaining the focus of intervention, should be of interest to most practitioners of short-term treatment. Our arguments concerning the rapidity of problem change, the natural limitations of professional intervention, and the motivating effects of time limits, offer a rationale for all modes of brief treatment. At this level the volume is an effort to synthesize in a form useful for caseworkers a range of formulations and findings relating to short-term methods.

Such a synthesis must be fairly general, however, since

short-term practice comprises a great diversity of methods. While there may be something to be gained by an analysis of the generic aspects of short-term casework, it is important to recognize that these aspects are confined largely to the structure of treatment. To designate a model of casework practice as brief and time-limited says certain things about it and implies others, but does not describe it very fully. In fact, one might say that planned brevity provides the form but not the substance of treatment. It simply offers us a medium with which to build more economical and perhaps sounder models of service. If this medium is to be used to full advantage, we must then turn to the construction of particular models of short-term practice. In short, we must develop the substance of this practice: the ways in which a limited amount of therapeutic time can be best utilized to serve our clients.

This brings us to the second and perhaps central purpose of the book: to set forth a particular system of short-term casework. We have attempted to construct a treatment design with a wide range of applications. In fact, it is offered for use with most clients normally served by caseworkers. We have deliberately opted for breadth over depth, since we think there is special need for a generic model of short-term practice. In so doing, we sacrifice the advantages of specificity that would be gained in developing a treatment approach for a particular type of problem or one featuring a particular mode of intervention. But we hope there are compensating gains in providing practitioners and agencies with a model that may be used across a variety of cases and in conjunction with a range of techniques.

Our system of treatment is presented through a framework which sets forth certain requirements for treatment systems in general. The framework is developed primarily to help us sort out and order the various elements in our system. It has served, we think, to make more explicit both the substance and limits of this system. Hopefully, it will serve as a guide for the future development of this system and will prove useful in the analysis, evaluation, and improvement of other systems as well.

A third purpose of the book is to present a set of ideas that may be of interest and use to caseworkers regardless of where they stand in respect to short-term treatment in general or our version in particular. Since we take the position that planned short-term treatment should be the dominant form of case-work, we must address ourselves to questions concerning casework in general. Moreover, many of the formulations we present about short-term casework have more general application. We do not subscribe to the notion that a given treatment design must be carried out in a unified way in order to make a useful contribution. Most experienced casework practitioners, we think, build their own models of practice in a rather eclectic manner, and we see no point in contesting this fact. While we come prepared to argue the case for the application of our approach in its entirety, we are also willing to concede that its greatest contribution may lie in selective use of its components.

The final purpose of the book is to develop two types of linkages between casework practice and research. One type concerns the utilization by caseworkers of a sizable and growing body of research relevant to casework practice. Some of this research has been conducted on casework itself. Much more has involved studies of psychotherapy, and even greater amounts consist of investigations of human behavior that bear directly or indirectly upon treatment questions. It is true that the usefulness of much of this research, even studies of case-work, begins to fade when we reach the sticking-point of ap-plication to actual cases. But it is also true that our efforts to make use of research in the service of casework practice have been not sufficiently systematic, thorough, or imaginative. While we do not intend in this volume to cover relevant re-search exhaustively, we do plan to connect formulations about practice to empirical moorings if they exist, and if they do not, to acknowledge their absence as a deficit in knowledge.

The other kind of linkage between research and practice that we wish to explicate may ultimately provide a more pow-erful means of improving practice. We are referring to the use of research as an integral means of developing and testing models of practice. With the possible exceptions of the Rogeri-ans and the behavioral therapists, there has been little effort to put research to work in a systematic way to improve treat-ment designs. What we advocate, and plan to demonstrate, is the collection of research data on cases treated according to a given model and the use of feedback from the data to modify the model.

FRAMEWORK: THE ELEMENTS OF A TREATMENT SYSTEM

We aim to accomplish our various purposes through setting forth a formal system of intervention—task-centered case-work. The presentation will directly achieve the central objec-tive of the book, to set forth a particular design for short-term treatment. At the same time, the treatment system will serve as a vehicle for conveying our thoughts about short-term methods, about casework in general, and about connections between research and treatment.

In working on this system we have found it useful to think of the attributes of *systems of interpersonal treatment* in general, that is, treatment systems, such as casework, counseling, or psychotherapy, in which the active ingredients are found within the communications that occur between practitioners and recipients. Through this means we have derived a framework for the presentation of our own system as well as certain criteria by which to assess the adequacy of our treatment design at its current stage of development.

There have been several efforts to develop frameworks for the comparative study of schools of psychotherapy (Harper, 1959; Ford and Urban, 1963; Patterson, 1966), and one recent attempt to do the same for the various approaches used in casework (Roberts and Nee, 1970). Our notion of what constitutes a treatment system draws from these contributions but uses no particular one as a prototype. As we see it, any treatment system has a certain anatomy consisting at least of the following elements: a treatment model; a supporting theory; an empirical base; and a set of value premises. The nature of these elements will now be considered.

THE TREATMENT MODEL. A system of treatment may be viewed as being built around a treatment model. In our terminology a model is a coherent set of directives which state how a given kind of treatment is to be carried out. A model is basically definitional and descriptive. It usually states what the practitioner is expected to do or what practitioners customarily do under given conditions. Casework models normally include some delineation of the kinds of problem or disorder for which they are intended, methods of diagnosis and assessment, desired ways of relating to clients, and statements of treatment goals, strategies, and techniques.

Such models may be characterized along a number of dimensions. First, models vary in respect to the type of target at which treatment is aimed. Thus in Perlman's (1970) problem-solving model, the target is viewed as the psychosocial problem; in Thomas's (1970) behavior modification approach, the target is specific behavior; or in Scherz's (1970) conception of family treatment, it consists of disturbed family interaction.

The target of a model may encompass a wide range of specific problems. If so, the model may be said to be *general* in scope. Perlman's problem-solving and Hollis's (1970) psychosocial approaches are examples of general models. At the other end of the continuum are *specialized* models confined to a very limited range of disorders. Here we find models designed for treatment of specific problems, such as school phobias or clients in a particular diagnostic category, such as the "borderline" client. Often such models are developed within the framework of general models. In fact they may be largely extensions or specifications of more comprehensive approaches.

A basic assumption of architects of general models is that certain fundamental principles can be successfully applied to a broad range of situations and therein, of course, lies their appeal. A practitioner need not master a large assortment of approaches to cope with the variety of cases he is likely to encounter but rather can rely on variations of a single approach. But because of their very generality such models may suffer from vagueness and lack of specific guidelines. Also there is the risk of a poor fit between the model and various kinds of case situations, as may happen, for example, when a Rogerian counselor encounters a non-verbal client or when a behavior therapist deals with a highly complex psychosocial problem.

Specialized models essentially sacrifice scope in order to obtain better fits to the requirements of particular targets. While it may be more feasible to develop highly specific guidelines in specialized models, specificity is not a necessary requirement. A model may have a narrow scope but its directives may still be quite unspecific.

Second, models differ according to the extent to which contingencies confronting the practitioner are taken into account. An undifferentiated model basically designates a change target and suggests a course of intervention. While both the target and intervention may be described in detail, such a model does not answer the question "what if"; that is, it does not state how treatment should be modified if the client has a particular diagnosis or what range of options are available if the client reacts in a given way to the practitioner's efforts. The model may incorporate some all-purpose contingency clause to the effect that what is done depends on the case, or some such; but if it lacks a statement of what precisely is to be done in respect to what kind of case, then the model remains undifferentiated. Obviously, lack of differentiation must be seen as a shortcoming of a model, since it provides no guidelines to help the practitioner cope with variations encountered in practice. No model can be expected to cover every contingency. Even in well-developed models, such as Hollis's psychosocial approach, differentiation is only partially and unevenly achieved. The need for differentiation depends somewhat on the model's target. For example, a specialized model designed for a homogenous population may not require a great deal of differentiation, since the amount of possible variation is limited from the outset.

Finally, models vary in respect to the amount of information conveyed by their statements. "Information" is used here in a sense similar to its meaning in information theory (Parry, 1967). A statement conveying a high degree of information is one that leaves the practitioner with little uncertainty of how to act in conformity with the model. For example, in short-term treatment models the expected duration of service may be specified in terms of a particular number of interviews, say six or twelve. In carrying out the model, the practitioner, rightly or wrongly, proceeds with greater certitude than if the duration of service was said to be dependent upon the "needs of the client."

Most statements in most models (and perhaps ours is no exception) have a relatively low information yield. Terms employed may be so vague and ambiguous that the practitioner gets little sense of what is expected. He may be told that "establishing a relationship" or "treatment alliance" is the first order of business in working with a client, but may be given no clear idea how this is to be done.

Often statements in treatment models are expressed in terms of possible action the practitioner might pursue in a given situation. Such statements usually contain such qualifiers as "may," "often," or "sometimes." An excerpt from Scherz's model (1970) provides a good example:

When treatment continues beyond symptomatic relief or crisis resolution, other techniques may assume greater proportion and significance. There is *likely* to be less dealing with the what, how, and effects of interpersonal behavior and more interpretation of underlying motives. There *probably* will be less directive activity.

. . . There *may be* more interpretation of the meaning of individual conflicts to the person and the family. . . . Interpretation of resistance and transference phenomena *often* become the main technique. (p. 247; italics added)

Statements of this sort obviously provide only limited information, although they do reduce uncertainty to some extent by suggesting possible courses of action. At this stage of the art, much model writing in social work must of necessity be at this level. It is important, however, to keep in mind that at this level the amount of direction provided by the model is slight.

The informational level of a model usually varies considerably from component to component and from phase to phase. In general models offer firmer guidelines in the initial than in subsequent phases. This is not surprising since the number of possible contingencies to be dealt with multiply rapidly after the beginning of treatment. In a similar vein and for similar reasons, rules of strategy in complex games, like bridge or chess, are much better developed for openings than middles.

Treatment models provide, at best, incomplete statements of the events with which they are concerned. In attempting to follow a model the practitioner often encounters "unmarked areas," in which paths and sign-posts are lacking. These areas, which may reflect gaps in general knowledge or in knowledge available to the theoretician, are preferable to arbitrary or misleading directives. No advantage is gained from premature completeness.

A SUPPORTING THEORY. A treatment model is descriptive and prescriptive rather than analytic: it sets forth a certain way of conceptualizing and ordering practice. It answers the question of "what" and "how" but not "why." The latter question is the province of theory supporting the model. As Lewis (1971) puts it:

Theory in social work is intended to provide explanations for the phenomena of practice. These explanations give reasons for the phenomena behaving in the way they do and being what they are. Rules and principles . . . serve as reasons for the social worker doing what he does but do not explain the why of his action. This latter explanation ultimately rests with the theories that justify such rules and principles. (p. 16)

The theory of a treatment system consists primarily of a set of assumptions and hypotheses which provide a rationale for the treatment model and explanations of its operations. In addition, theory provides the practitioner with hypotheses which he may use as a basis for making practice decisions in situations for which the model offers no clear guidelines.

At its core, treatment theory consists of formulations about: 1) the etiology and causes of the problems to which the model is addressed; and 2) the effects of the different kinds of intervention proposed by the model. These formulations are related to larger bodies of theory that also may be drawn on. Thus systems of casework practice have traditionally leaned strongly on personality theory, particularly psychoanalytic variations. In recent years increasing use has been made of other types of theory, including learning theory, crisis theory, small group theory, and organizational theory. In some cases the connection between a treatment system and a body of supporting theory is strong and explicit, as it is between Thomas's behavior modification (1970) and learning theory or between Hollis's psychosocial approach and psychoanalytic theories of personality. In other cases connections are less tight. A treatment theorist may choose, for example, to take an eclectic position toward a class of theory—as Perlman appears to do in relating her problem-solving model to personality theory. Such openness in respect to supporting theory increases the amount of uncertainty in the system but at the same time permits greater flexibility in use of theory by the practitioners of the model. All treatment systems bear loose and indirect relations to various kinds of behavioral science theories, those which may be relevant to only certain aspects of a system or those that support theories which in turn support the treatment system.

Generally no distinction is made between "theory" and "model" in the literature on treatment systems. As a result rather different orders of abstractions are thrown together in a way which, on the surface, seems to simplify matters but ultimately, we think, leads to confusion. Perhaps some examples will serve to make clearer what we mean by this distinction.

In the casework literature one finds the principle that techniques designed to develop the client's insight into the dynamics of his behavior should be avoided or used sparingly with clients who may be classified as schizophrenic or "borderline" (Reid, 1964). Emphasis should rather be on "reality oriented" techniques such as advice giving, guidance, and the like. These are clearly "model" statements, since they suggest how the practitioner is to proceed in a given situation. The statements are related to certain theoretical hypotheses which may or may not be stated. Thus one relevant hypothesis would be that use of insight-oriented techniques with schizophrenic clients will result in elevation of their anxiety. The theoretical hypothesis provides a rationale for the treatment principle but does not state what this principle should be. As any hypothesis in a theory, it conveys no directives for action.

Model statements may not necessarily be related to theoretical hypotheses. The suggested length of an interview in a model may be fifty minutes, but there may be no theoretical justification for this. Conversely, theoretical formulations in the treatment system may lack analogs in the model. For example, in psychoanalytically oriented systems of treatment, there is usually a far greater amount of theory to explain why clients behave in certain ways toward their practitioners than there are corresponding treatment principles for dealing with such behavior. In such circumstances the practitioner is required to develop his own *modus operandi* from the theoretical formulations. Since theory statements may be used to "fill out" a model in this way, the distinction between theory and model may not be clearly drawn in the exposition of treatment systems. But this is all the more reason, we think, to make the distinction. To do so permits us to ask a number of critical questions of the system: What theoretical hypotheses are there in support of any given statement of the model? If there are none, what other justification is there for the statement? Does the theory suggest additional strategies and techniques for the model?

AN EMPIRICAL BASIS. The empirical base of a treatment system consists of data relating to the operations of its model or the validity of its theoretical hypotheses. These data come in a variety of forms including case records, clinical observations reported in the literature, and findings from formal studies. Regardless of their form or quality, all such data share one essential characteristic: they are, or purport to be, statements of events that have taken place. Whether one reports a large number of events from a single case or one event each from several hundred, one is making empirical statements.

Unlike theory statements they offer no explanations; unlike statements of a model, they convey no expectations. They are concerned with the raw facts of experience.

The empirical base of a model may be seen as a series of concentric circles. At its core are data collected for the purpose of testing the model's operations or its underlying theory. While this portion of the base is the most relevant to the model, it is usually the smallest. It is surrounded by a much larger circle which includes data from studies of similar models or of phenomena with which the model is directly concerned. These circles are surrounded by a third which comprises the broad field of behavioral research.

In order for data in the outer rings to be considered as part of the empirical base, however, they must be organized in relation to the model. Thus a model may rest on certain hypotheses concerning family interaction. Data from a range of studies on family treatment and family life may be germane to these hypotheses but the data would need to be systematically ordered in relation to the hypotheses. It is not enough simply to assert that findings from this or that kind of research support this or that kind of treatment approach.

VALUE PREMISES. The directives that constitute a treatment model are ultimately rooted in explicit or implicit value assumptions. The connection between a treatment operation and its value premise may be obscured by theoretical and empirical considerations, but it usually can be traced. For example, a model may call for the practitioner to help the client develop insight into the sources of his anxieties. This directive may be based on a theoretical hypothesis that an understanding of the causes of one's anxiety will lead to its diminution. But the theoretical hypothesis does not tell us why the anxiety should be reduced instead of left alone or increased. The answer ultimately lies in the realm of values. The reduction of the anxiety is assumed to be *desirable,* either in its own right or because it is expected to produce desirable consequences —improve mental health for example.

Virtually all value dimensions of concern to man influence treatment systems in one way or another. We will concentrate on three such dimensions that appear to be central in systems of casework. They all concern the practitioner's position vis-à-vis his clients and relate specifically to values placed on: 1) the client's own expressed wishes; 2) the worker's notions of what the client "needs" or what is "good" for him; 3) the protection of the interests of others as the worker sees them—the community, the family, or other individuals. Most value issues and premises concerning the caseworker's relations to his clients can be described along these dimensions or at points of conflict among them.

Each dimension has both quantitative and qualitative aspects. Quantitatively one can think of the extent to which one values what the client wants, what one wants for the client or what one deems to be the interest of others. The qualitative aspects are more complex. Different kinds of wishes of the client may be valued differently. Conceptions of what is "good" for the client may be organized around any number of themes; for example, we may think the client should not have to suffer abusive relationships or should not be allowed to commit suicide. Our concerns about protecting others will vary according to the kind of group or persons we have in mind and according to the nature of the threat to them.

When these dimensions are juxtaposed, value conflicts inevitably arise. A commitment to helping the client realize his own desires may conflict with our conception of what he needs or our concern for the interests of others. A sick, elderly man who wants our assistance in finding a room may place us in a quandary if we think he needs institutional care. A psychiatric patient's request that we help him secure a discharge may clash with our concern that he may not be able to control his aggressive impulses. What we think is good for the client may be at odds with our protective obligations. The individual welfares of two parents might profit from a separation but the possible effect their break-up might have on their four young children gives us pause.

Individual practitioners doubtless vary in "basic" positions on these value dimensions; for example, some may be characteristically more committed than others to carrying out the client's wishes. It may be, although we have no way of knowing, that such individual differences are less important than organizational and situational factors in determining how these dimensions will be applied.

Such complexities have not been dealt with in much detail in systems of casework. This is not surprising in view of the many conceptual difficulties and philosophical issues embedded in the subject and in view of the great amount of time and attention that must go into model construction. This explanation is also meant to serve as an apology in advance for the limitations in our treatment of value premises.

In most systems of treatment (including ours) value positions are stated at high levels of abstraction, without much specification. The client's "right to self-determination" may be reaffirmed but with the qualification that the caseworker may have to exercise his authority if the client acts in ways that may be harmful to himself or others. Seldom is it made clear what client actions may be considered harmful. Without this kind of specification, statements of value premises are little more than platitudes. There is usually little disagreement with them; there is also usually little agreement on what they really mean.

Problems of value dilemmas are usually glossed over. The naive reader is apt to come away with the notion, almost always erroneous, that the system rests on a set of well-integrated value premises. It would be far better to define the kinds of value conflict that may arise and to offer the practitioner some guidelines for coping with them.

Since value questions tend to be treated superficially, many of the value premises—often the more important ones—underlying a treatment system may never be exposed to the light of analysis. For example, values which dictate what we consider to be good for clients are seldom examined as such. We are apt to assume that such states as "mental health" and "optimal social functioning" represent ideals that clients naturally wish to attain. These notions are based, however, on our conceptions of what is desirable for the client and hence are reflections of value premises. The client may or may not share them.

There are, of course, other value dimensions that have an important bearing upon treatment systems. As Hellenbrand (1961) has suggested and as Turner (1964) has demonstrated empirically, the client's and practitioner's view of human nature, time, activity, and man's relations to nature and to others—the value orientations comprising Kluckhohn's (1958) well known paradigm—can affect transactions in casework. Another kind of dimension occurs in relation to values placed on different sources of knowledge, a subject that will be taken up in greater detail in the next chapter.

Our analysis was meant to be illustrative rather than exhaustive. Whatever the dimension considered, one seldom finds explicit, detailed statements of value premises in systems of casework.

CHAPTER TWO

A TREATMENT SYSTEM

In this chapter we shall present an overview and assessment of task-centered casework. The system in detail will be set forth in subsequent chapters.

THE TREATMENT MODEL

The model is designed for use with the majority of clients currently served by social caseworkers. The targets to which the model is addressed are problems of: 1) interpersonal conflict, 2) dissatisfaction in social relations, 3) relations with formal organizations, 4) role performance, 5) social transition, 6) reactive emotional distress, and 7) inadequate resources. The target problem must be one that the client expresses willingness to work on and is able to act on either independently or through the caseworker as his agent. Further, the problem must be limited to specific behaviors or circumstances.

Problems perceived by the client are elicited, explored, and clarified by the caseworker in the initial interview. The problem which the client is most anxious to resolve is normally seen as the primary target of intervention, if it meets the criteria of the model. If the client does not acknowledge a problem that would provide an acceptable target of intervention, the practitioner attempts to determine if one is present through a systematic review with the client of possible problem areas. If a target problem is not located through this process within the first two interviews, or in some cases through a more extended problem-search carried out with the explicit agreement of the client, there is no further basis for work with the client within the framework of the model. Assuming a target problem can be located, the practitioner and client reach agreement on the problem(s) to which their work will be addressed.

Once agreement on the problem has been reached, tasks are formulated and selected in collaboration with the client, in the first interview if possible. A task defines what the client is to do to alleviate his problem. The task represents both an immediate goal the client is to pursue and the means of achieving the larger goal of problem alleviation. In its initial formulation, a task provides a general statement of the action the client is to undertake rather than a detailed blueprint. For example, Mrs. Brown is to develop a firmer, more consistent approach in handling her child's behavior; Mr. and Mrs. Clark are to develop a plan for the care of their mentally retarded daughter. More than one task may be developed and worked on in a given course of treatment.

In general, the client's task is based on the course of action he thinks would be most effective in alleviating his problem.

The caseworker may then help the client modify the task to make it more focused and manageable. If the client is unable to propose an appropriate course of action, the caseworker helps the client develop a task through exploration and discussion of task possibilities which the caseworker may draw from the client or suggest himself. The task is so structured that chances of its being accomplished, in whole or in part, are high. Consequently the caseworker is able to convey realistic positive expectations that the client will be successful in carrying out the task.

Once the task has been explicitly formulated and agreed upon, the caseworker and client decide on the approximate amount and duration of service. In most cases eight to twelve interviews are planned to take place during a period of two to four months. Interviews generally occur at weekly intervals though the frequency may vary.

Once an agreement has been reached on the nature of the client's task and the limits of service, the caseworker's interventions are then directed almost exclusively toward helping the client accomplish the agreed-upon task. As treatment proceeds, the task may be revised, usually in the direction of greater specificity. In some cases the task may be completely reformulated or new tasks added.

The model contains no "diagnostic phase." The practitioner continually makes diagnostic judgments which both guide and are guided by his activities. These judgments are first concerned with classification, specification, and exploration of the clients' problems; then with assessment of possible client tasks and finally with evaluation of his efforts to achieve tasks agreed upon. In general the practitioner attempts to be both systematic and responsive in his communications to the client.

Thus he tries to focus communication in order to accomplish agreed upon goals but in a manner that conveys interest and empathic understanding and in a way that builds upon the client's own communications. Specific types of communication include: 1) exploration of the client's problem, task possibilities, and task-related behavior; 2) structuring the treatment relationship and communication within it; 3) enhancing the client's awareness in ways to help him overcome obstacles to, or otherwise facilitate, task achievement; 4) encouragement of task-directed behavior; and 5) suggesting means of task accomplishment. Comparable types of communication are used when family members are interviewed together or in work with individuals on the clients' behalf. The caseworker's operations, whether carried out with the clients or with others, are used in whatever combination will best help the client achieve the task in the most direct and economical way possible.

The process of terminating treatment is begun in the initial phase when the duration of treatment is set. In the last, or next-to-last interview, the client is helped to identify his achievements, apply what he has done to remaining problems, and define future tasks he might undertake on his own. Extensions beyond agreed-upon limits are made only in exceptional cases and then usually for brief, specified periods.

This treatment design is offered as an addition to the relatively small number of casework models, and to the relatively large number of models of interpersonal treatment. As we have seen, it contains few elements that are really new, and nothing that is revolutionary. Its *raison d'être* lies in the particular synthesis that we have tried to achieve.

As a brief, time-limited service aimed at specific problems, the present approach belongs to a general class of models of short-term, interpersonal treatment. It differs from most psychotherapeutic approaches in respect to both target problems and methods of intervention. While the target problems of task-centered casework and those of models of brief psychotherapy share a good deal of common ground, there are important differences in range. Our model excludes certain disorders, such as phobias and psychophysiological problems to which brief psychotherapy models may be addressed. On the other hand, we include certain psychosocial difficulties, such as problems of relations with formal organizations and of inadequate resources, that are generally not seen as targets of short-term psychotherapy. Our range of intervention is somewhat broader, covering practitioner activities in the client's social network. Quite possibly (though this remains to be demonstrated) there are also differences in emphasis given to various types of interventions. We would expect, for example, that in task-centered casework there would be relatively greater use of direction, encouragement, and techniques to help clients increase their understanding of others and their social situations; there would probably be less use of methods designed to promote the client's awareness of the dynamics of his own behavior. In these respects, we think, the present approach incorporates certain characteristics that differentiate casework from psychotherapy models generally.

But how does this approach differ from existing models of planned short-term casework? Among the more common models was the one used in a previous study conducted by the senior author (Reid and Shyne, 1969). Families with relational problems were seen for a maximum of eight interviews following a brief study phase. Focal problems, usually segments of some larger family difficulty, were identified and limited goals relating to these problems were pursued. Aside from the durational limits, the treatment design was left rather vague. To a large extent, it was a matter of seeing how much could be accomplished if the span of treatment were arbitrarily limited. Approaches of this sort typify much of the practice of planned, short-term casework.

The present model has evolved from the short-term treatment design just described. In the course of its evolution, certain elements have been added, including the problem typology, the stress on an explicit worker-client agreement on the objectives of treatment, the organization of treatment goals and methods around client tasks, and the specification of modes of intervention. There are also differences other than additions. Diagnosis is centered around the target problems and tasks rather than the client's personality traits or functioning. Through the use of the task construct, treatment goals are made more specific and limited. That is, the goal is not to try to make as much headway as one can on some problem within a stated number of sessions, but rather to help the client carry out a specified course of action. In general more credence is given to the client's own conception of the problem and his own plan for solution.

Many of these distinctions hold when task-centered casework is compared to still other short-term casework models. We are often asked how our approach differs from "crisis intervention." It is a question difficult to answer, since this rubric usually refers to no specific model but rather to a diversity of approaches intimately or loosely concerned with human crises of one sort or another. It is possible, however, to compare our approach with particular casework models based on crisis theory, such as those developed by Parad (1963) and Rapoport (1970). Our work certainly reflects the thinking of these crisis theorists. Our model is somewhat more inclusive since it is not confined to treatment of crises; moreover it places greater emphasis on specification of target problem, client tasks and time limits.

There are certain parallels between the present model and the "functional" approaches to casework. Smalley (1967, 1971) has been the major exponent of this point of view in recent years. Taking her version of this approach for purposes of comparison, we find that our use of time limits, our stress on client self-direction in the use of help, and the importance we attach to the use of structure and focus in casework, are in accord with the functional model. Functional casework, as viewed by Smalley at least, is not necessarily short-term, although use is made of time limits to establish boundaries for the caseworker-client relationship. The theoretical bases of task-centered casework are more diversified and we give greater weight to the products of formal research on casework and psychotherapy. Classifications of target problems and treatment techniques do not appear in Smalley's work, while such typologies are the backbone of our model. Finally, we place less stress on the agency's "function" as a determinant of the kind of help to be offered.

Task-centered casework also bears certain similarities to at least two major casework approaches which are not, strictly speaking, either short-term or time limited, namely models developed by Perlman (1957, 1970) and Hollis (1964, 1970). Our conceptualization of change targets as problems, our use of the client's problem as the main focus for diagnosis, and our procedures for problem-exploration, constitute points of resemblance to Perlman's problem-solving approach. In these respects, as well as others, we have been influenced by Perlman's work. Our model differs from hers in respect to such aspects as duration, scope and methods of treatment, and planning of termination. While task-centered casework differs in fundamental respects from Hollis's psychosocial approach, our conceptualization of the practitioner's methods of treatment owes much to her classification of casework procedures (Hollis, 1964, 1967).*

It may be useful to assess the present model in respect to certain of its formal characteristics. Clearly task-centered casework is a general, rather than specialized, model. Existing models of short-term casework and psychotherapy tend to have more limited targets. We thought there was need for a more comprehensive model of brief treatment, and hence we opted for breadth rather than depth.

As will be seen in the next chapter, we stake out something less than the total array of problems that caseworkers are called upon to deal with. Nevertheless the set of problems to which we address ourselves covers a broad and diverse range. We must accept the limitations inherent in general models. We cannot, for example, specify in detail how one might characterize and treat any *particular* type of problem, as would be done if we were presenting a specialized model. At its present stage of development our model is not well differentiated, as we have previously defined the term. Although certain contingencies are taken into account (the client who does not recognize a problem, for example) we have not yet developed in any detail treatment strategies specific to different problem

---

* A fuller background against which our system can be examined is provided by Simon (1970) in her comparative analysis of major systems of casework.

categories. Our only comfort at this point is that the degree of differentiation in most general treatment models is not much better.

A SUPPORTING THEORY

The present model is based most directly on formulations about the processes and limits of change characteristic of the target problems within its domain. It is hypothesized that such problems typically reflect temporary breakdowns in problem coping which trigger corrective change forces. These forces, the most important of which is the individual's drive for change, operate quickly to reduce the problem to a tolerance level, at which point their intensity diminishes and the possibility of further change lessens. Brief treatment designs better fit these change processes than long term approaches, since most of the change in a target problem is likely to occur within the time period spanned by brief treatment. Setting limits in advance may serve to augment and quicken these processes of change by providing a deadline against which the client must work and by heightening his expectancy that certain changes can occur within the period allotted. The caseworker's role is to guide, focus and stimulate these change forces. This role can be discharged most effectively through a concentrated effort on helping the client carry out some sequence of behaviors, or task, designed to bring about change in his problem.

The nature of the caseworker's contribution to change can be set out in a series of hypotheses: one set of hypotheses posits that the presence of certain qualities of caseworker communication, such as the degree to which it is responsive and systematic, will be associated with task accomplishment and problem alleviation. Another set posits that use of specific interventions, such as enhancing the client's awareness, will result in demonstrable change in his behavior or his social field and ultimately will further task achievement. Still another set posits a connection between task accomplishment and problem change. Through such hypotheses the various kinds of caseworker inputs described in the model are linked to given outcomes.

The theory which our treatment system formally encompasses at this point consists of a relatively small number of propositions. Two other uses of theory are made, however. First, most of the theoretical constructs and propositions we have developed are either drawn from or related to larger bodies of theory including general systems theory, communication theory, role theory, psychoanalytic theory, and certain theories of learning. It is expected that practitioners using the system can draw from these theories other propositions compatible with those in our system. Second, our model contains a number of open areas which practitioners may find necessary to fill through recourse to certain bodies of knowledge. For example, while we direct the practitioner to make diagnostic judgments about the origins of the client's problems, we specify no one system that might be used to help him form such judgments. Similarly we offer no theory of personality development or functioning to explain the client's behavior. Thus let us suppose a client has problems concerning her depression over having given birth to a mongoloid infant, compounded by conflicts with the hospital staff. A practitioner using our model to help this client might use psychoanalytic theories of maternal reactions to births of defective children, crisis theory, theories of depression and organizational theory.

Some treatment models are tied to particular and extensive

bodies of formal theory concerning human development and functioning. For example, psychoanalytic models have their roots in Freudian psychodynamics, in latter day ego psychology and the like; and behavior modification models are closely linked to theories of learning. By comparison the formal theoretical base of our model is both more diversified and less extensive. It is so for reasons that have to do with our conception of the nature of casework and its knowledge base. Perhaps the most distinguishing characteristic of casework, if indeed it has any, is its dual focus on psychological and social phenomena. We have yet to develop an adequate body of theory that integrates these foci. Thus the caseworker must make a choice on the one hand between a basic commitment to some body of theory that in effect neglects important aspects of this complex psychosocial field or on the other, a position of theoretical pluralism that enables him to utilize whatever formal theories are relevant to his purposes. We think the latter alternative is more viable. Moreover, we have misgivings about the utility of most formal theories that might be called upon to support a system of casework treatment. We agree with Kurt Lewin that nothing is as practical as a good theory but would add that a good theory in this field is hard to find.

As caseworkers we have, of course, our old standby—psychoanalytic theory—in its manifold forms. It is a theory that has contributed much to casework and will continue to do so. Since both authors of this volume were raised in this theoretical tradition, our own system certainly bears its imprint. Still we must bear in mind that psychoanalytically based models of casework have yet to prove their efficacy and psychoanalytic theory itself has serious shortcomings, including its reliance upon propositions that are difficult to test, the imprecision of its language, and its general lack of empirical verification. Certain learning theories present impressive empirical credentials and the promise of considerable value for casework but in our judgment need further development before they can be useful in helping practitioners deal with complex psychosocial problems which require more than change in very specific behaviors. Certain other bodies of "theory" (such as role theory and systems theory) that have been suggested as supports for casework are more descriptive than explanatory. They are basically conceptual schemes. Unless a theory contains propositions that attempt to *explain* psychological and social phenomena, its value as a base for a treatment system is quite limited. From such conceptual schemes one obtains fruitful ways of viewing phenomena and we make use of them for this purpose, but they do not take us very far along the road toward understanding the dynamics of psychological and social events.

In view of these considerations we decided not to tie our model to any formal bodies of theory but rather to let the practitioner make use of whatever supporting theories he might choose. The theoretical base we have developed for the model is admittedly lean and needs this kind of supplementation, but we would rather have it this way than to make a commitment to a theory of limited range or questionable quality. Our strategy is to expand our theoretical base through our own research and through incorporation of empirically supported propositions from the behavior sciences in general.

There are obvious drawbacks to this position since we do not provide practitioners with all the theoretical guidelines they might expect from a treatment system and ask them in addition to locate and integrate relevant theories in their use of the model. Nonetheless our position does accord with certain trends in social work. In both casework practice and in the graduate education of caseworkers there seems to be a movement away from a primary reliance on psychoanalytic theory or psychoanalytic models of practice toward use of a plurality of theoretical systems and practice approaches. Increasingly casework students, who will be the practitioners of the future, are being exposed to a range of points of view about behavior and treatment. The student is expected to take more responsibility for putting together this diversity of inputs in a way that makes sense to him. This kind of education should prepare him well for using models such as ours.

These observations should not be taken to mean that we intend the model to be used only by practitioners with graduate training. We must recognize that most caseworkers engaged in direct practice do not have advanced degrees; moreover, to an increasing extent preparation for practice is being provided at undergraduate levels (Pins, 1971). Our permissive position in respect to supporting theories enables the model to be used by practitioners who do not have the kind of extensive theoretical knowledge provided at the graduate level. In fact our most extensive test of the model thus far (reported in the final chapter) was conducted among practitioners who were just beginning graduate training. We would expect, however, that the model would be used for different purposes and at different levels by practitioners with differing amounts and kinds of education. Caseworkers with graduate training might use the model to help clients carry out tasks requiring changes in complex patterns of behavior, attitudes, and feelings—tasks likely to be derived from problems of interpersonal conflict, dissatisfactions in social relations, role performance, and reactive emotional distress. To help clients effectively with such tasks may require the kind of knowledge of behavioral theory customarily taught in Master's programs in social work; in any event we assume that such knowledge, at whatever level it might be obtained, would enhance the caseworker's performance with these types of tasks. Caseworkers with less knowledge of behavioral theory should be able to apply the model effectively to most problems of inadequate resources, social transition, and relations with formal organizations; and perhaps to some problems of reactive emotional distress. They may also be able to use the model to help clients carry out less complex tasks derived from the remaining problems.

AN EMPIRICAL BASIS

The empirical basis of task-centered casework at its present stage of development is largely in previous research on casework, counseling, and psychotherapy. Particular stress has been placed on a large number of studies of the outcomes of treatment, both short and long term. From this mass of evidence certain empirical generalizations can be derived: 1) recipients of brief, time-limited treatment show at least as much durable improvement as recipients of long-term, open-ended treatment; 2) most of the improvement associated with long-term treatment occurs relatively soon after treatment has begun; 3) regardless of their intended length, most courses of treatment turn out to be relatively brief. These generalizations, elaborated upon and applied in different ways, are the main support for our thesis that models like ours are generally more useful than long-term, open-ended approaches. Other kinds of findings derived from this body of research as well as from other studies of interpersonal treatment provide empirical support for specific approaches called for by the model.

In addition, we have accumulated a modest amount of data on the operation of the task-centered model itself, mostly in the form of case records and client responses to questionnaires. These data have emerged from clinical trials of the model, conducted primarily in medical and psychiatric settings. The trials have been conducted chiefly for developmental purposes: to test its feasibility and range of application, to locate problems, to generate ideas about how it might be improved. While outcome data have been obtained in the process, no attempt has yet been made to conduct a definitive test of its effectiveness.

At this point the empirical base for the model lies primarily in evidence for hypotheses on which the model depends. Thus results of research are used to support the proposition that change in target problems tends to occur rapidly and this proposition in turn underlies the short-term features of our treatment design. In few instances, however, can conclusive evidence be shown for such propositions. Moreover, proof that different components of a model may work well is not proof that the model as a whole operates successfully.

Short-term models such as ours derive support from the general finding that individuals appear to derive as much benefit from brief as they do from long-term treatment. This evidence is important in relation to questions concerning which of the two modes of treatment is preferable, but does not establish that either form is clearly preferable to no treatment at all. Nor does this evidence offer a basis for assessing short-term treatment against some form of treatment, such as behavior therapy, that differs substantially from the standard models of long-term casework and psychotherapy that have been used as a basis for comparison.

Although we wish to be explicit about the limitations of our scientific base, we do not intend to be excessively self-critical. Very few models of interpersonal treatment receive much testing prior to their unveiling. In fact most are introduced relatively unencumbered by systematic evidence as to their effects.

VALUE PREMISES

The value premises of the present model fall within the general framework of values that guide the practice of casework in the United States. But within this framework we have attempted to develop a set of premises that may distinguish our approach from certain others. A focal construct of this value scheme is the client's expressed, considered request—what it is he says he wants after he has had a chance to consider his needs in relation to the caseworker's offerings. The practitioner's primary role is to serve as the agent to help clients satisfy their requests within limitations of his resources and skills, the mandate of his agency and the laws of the land. Thus a high value is placed on helping the client obtain what he asks for, even though we may have reservations about the worth of his requests, may regard other goals as more important or may even suspect that at some deeper level he "really" wants something else. To be sure, the practitioner has the right, and in some cases, the obligation to challenge the expressed request of the client, to make sure that the client has taken into account alternative courses and possible consequences; but the client's request, whatever form it may take after its examination, provides the goals for the caseworker's subsequent activity.

Furthermore, this set of values forecloses the practitioner from attempting to pursue goals that are not directly related to the client's request. The practitioner treats only those conditions the client has requested treatment for. This principle does not prevent the caseworker from attempting to elicit an "enabling request" from a client, but he respects the client's right to be informed about new or expanded treatment plans. As Gottlieb and Stanley (1966) have so aptly put it, goals in casework should be "consciously established and mutually agreed upon by client and worker" (p. 471).

This set of values is based on the assumption that a person who asks for help should be able to choose what he wants help with and what he does not. Moreover we assume that the choice he *expresses* has essential validity and is to be respected, regardless of our judgments about his intelligence, motivation, emotional state or unconscious strivings, or regardless of what we think may be in his best interests.

The role accorded research in our treatment system reflects rather different value premises. We hold that knowledge acquired through application of systematic methods of inquiry, that is through formal research, is of greater value than knowledge acquired through other means, including expert opinion, practice wisdom, uncontrolled observations or deductions from theory. We recognize the limitations in quantity and quality of available research-based knowledge and we also are aware that other forms of knowledge serve essential functions. But only through research-based knowledge, we think, can we develop progressively effective treatment models. Acceptance of this position should cause the practitioner to evaluate knowledge by strict criteria, for example to require that assertions be supported by systematic evidence before they are accepted as anything but tentative hypotheses. Since few assertions in any treatment system can pass such a test, the practitioner must realize that his knowledge base is uncertain at best. This orientation should be combined with a commitment to the use of research as a major means of generating knowledge for practice. We hope that practitioners who use our model would insist that sustained research activity, conducted by themselves or others, accompany their efforts.

We have so far identified only the more salient of the value premises that might distinguish our treatment system from others. Even in respect to these, it is difficult to make meaningful comparisons with other systems because of the semantic slipperiness of the whole subject. It is still possible, however, to distinguish our position from some other points of view one encounters among casework practitioners.

Many caseworkers (in common with many helping professionals) seem to regard their function as helping clients move toward some state defined by abstract values, such as mental health, family well-being, or the like. The specific request the client presents is accordingly not given great weight. It may be seen as a symptom of some larger disorder reflecting some deviation from the ideal state or as a point of entry to permit the practitioner to work toward some larger goal. This devaluing of the client's manifest request is further justified on the ground that the client's motivation to seek help is often unconsciously determined. Thus what the client says he wants may not be what he really wants at a deeper level. Because of his knowledge of unconscious processes and his objectivity, the clinician, according to this logic, may be in a better position to figure out the client's true motivation than the client himself!

This configuration of values (and supporting technique) reflect what might be called a "reformist" orientation toward helping. The practitioner is guided by certain overarching ideals that he hopes he can help his client achieve, at least in some measure. As a realist, he may not expect his efforts to enable his client to fully realize the ideal, whether it be mental health, emotional maturity, marital compatibility, or some other desired state, but the ideal is what he works toward. The lineage of the reformist orientation can be traced perhaps to the essentially religious origins of American casework (Reid, 1971). In its earliest days casework was a mixed offering of material assistance and moral upgrading. As Parad (1971) observes, "The goal of friendly visiting, precursor of casework, was moral rehabilitation, obviously a lengthy process" (p. 120).

Underlying the reformist position is the assumption that the practitioner is a better judge of what the client really needs than the client himself. It is an assumption that is usually expressed in subtle rather than obvious forms, and often as a technical principle rather than as a value judgment. Nonetheless it can be discerned, we think, in such examples as the following: a mother who asks for help in coping with the behavior of her child is ultimately viewed as a "borderline" personality who "needs" a stable relationship with a caseworker to make up for the emotional deprivation she endured as a child. An aged client who requests money from a private agency so she can visit her children is "really" asking for help (though she cannot express it) with difficulties in her relationship with them. A caseworker assists a "multiproblem" family to secure public housing in order to establish a relationship with the family which will enable the worker to help the family with other, presumably more serious, problems.

This value position can be defended on various grounds, but in our view it leads to a depreciation of the client's right to make his own decisions about his own problems. We are certainly aware that this issue contains far more complexities than we have dealt with here or can deal with in this book, but we did think it important to contrast a key value orientation underlying our model with a perhaps more prevalent orientation.

Our value position in respect to the importance of research-based knowledge has no formal counter-position—everybody is in favor of a scientific base!—but an opposing point of view is both expressed informally and acted out in behavior. Practitioners have exhibited notorious reluctance to utilize the findings of research, particularly when results run counter to accepted beliefs. It is not surprising that Rosenblatt (1968) found that caseworkers in a variety of settings placed research reports at the bottom of a listing of types of knowledge used in their practice.

Such observations can be partially explained on grounds that research has not yet offered enough "pay-off" to serve as an important resource for practitioners, but there is another and perhaps more critical explanation for practitioners' lack of interest in the results of research. It is perhaps that practitioners prefer knowledge that provides coherent, plausible explanations of phenomena encountered in practice situations. The apparent usefulness of the knowledge in solving practice problems is accorded greater weight than its empirical base. Knowledge of this type can be more readily supplied by the theoretical literature, supervisors, consultants, and practical experience than by research. Its usefulness, however, may be more apparent than real. It may provide the practitioner with a sense of security and purpose in his work but may not offer a base for effective practice. The history of the helping arts is replete with examples of bodies of unverified knowledge that inspired practitioners but did little good for those they were trying to help. Thus a vast fund of knowledge based on expert opinion and practical experience provided a foundation for blood-letting. We may smile today at the "depletion theory" of the eminent eighteenth-century American physician, Dr. Benjamin Rush, who was convinced that draining large quantities of blood was an effective therapy because it afforded relief to overexcited tissues, but practitioners of interpersonal treatment today are guided by theories that are no better supported by empirical data than was Dr. Rush's theory of depletion.

CHAPTER THREE

TARGET PROBLEMS

FOLLOWING the work of Helen Perlman (1957), we have taken the concept of "problem" to define the targets of change in our theoretical formulations. This model is addressed to what are often referred to as "problems of living." In our use of the expression we mean psychological and social problems that most of us encounter and cope with in some form in the normal course of existence. These are problems as the individual defines them and problems that can be resolved or alleviated through the individual's own actions. Such problems come to the attention of caseworkers when persons or families are unable to carry out effective problem-reducing actions on their own or through informal helpers. The general purpose of this model is to enable clients to accomplish such actions which, in the context of treatment, we refer to as "tasks."

A PROBLEM TYPOLOGY

We have developed a tentative typology to identify the major kinds of target problems our model addresses. Since the model itself is intended for use with most clients who come into contact with caseworkers, the problem typology is broad in scope. It lacks attributes of an ideal taxonomy, however. It is not exhaustive, distinctions among categories are not always clear, and it is not built on well-defined bases of classification. It seemed more sensible to try to conceptualize certain typical problems in a rough but useful way than to attempt to develop a more technically perfect but less practical scheme. It is important to keep in mind that we are attempting to classify problems, not clients. Obviously clients may have more than one problem in this scheme. Also our interest is in *target* problems, those difficulties to which casework intervention in our model is actually addressed.

We have identified seven major problem groupings.

INTERPERSONAL CONFLICT. In this broad category fall problems of conflict between specific individuals. Most commonly encountered are conflicts within families, between husband and wife, parent and child, or siblings; but caseworkers are also called upon to deal with conflicts outside of the family context, between teacher and pupil, doctor and patient, employer and employee, and the like. A client may, of course, be in conflict with more than one other person, as in a family in which conflict arises among several members. To avoid unnecessary complexity and vagueness, however, we prefer to view a given problem of conflict as existing between two individuals, recognizing that in some case situations more than one such problem can be identified.

Interpersonal conflict is then a problem occurring in the interaction between two individuals. At least one is behaving in a way the other finds objectionable. In most cases the behavior of each is unacceptable to the other. It is the essence of the problem, of course, that the two antagonists are bound together in a relationship from which neither can readily withdraw.

While conflict may have its source in the needs, personality characteristics, role expectations, and behavior of each participant, it cannot be properly understood in terms of these factors alone. It must be seen rather as the product of interaction between the participants, of how A behaves toward B, which in turn causes B to behave in a certain way toward A, and so on. Interpersonal conflicts are thus built through "vicious circles" whose exact origin is often undiscernible, and is usually irrelevant.

DISSATISFACTION IN SOCIAL RELATIONS. An individual may not be experiencing conflict with another, yet still may be troubled by certain aspects of his interpersonal relations. A problem of this kind is centered in the individual client rather than between two clients. The client usually perceives deficiencies or excesses in his interactions with others. For example, he may feel he is not sufficiently assertive, that he is excessively shy or dependent, or that he is overly aggressive. He may feel generally isolated and lonely. He may be dissatisfied with his relations with a particular group, such as members of the opposite sex or people in authority. Such problems are most likely to occur among single adults living apart from their families of origin, although they are by no means confined to this group. One family member may feel dissatisfied with his relations with another family member or other family members. Thus a woman may feel she is excessively vulnerable to her mother's criticisms. Normally some interpersonal conflict is a part of such a problem, but it may not be the most salient feature.

PROBLEMS WITH FORMAL ORGANIZATIONS. Problems of this type, like problems of interpersonal conflict, occur between the client and a specified other, although in the present instance the client's antagonist is more properly viewed as an organization rather than an individual. The client may find his interactions with individuals in the organization to be troublesome but their behavior is best viewed as an expression of an organizational position; that is, the client might expect to experience the same kind of difficulty with a different set of individuals occupying the same organizational slots.

A wide variety of problems of this sort come to the attention of social workers. An organization may not be providing services or resources to which the client is entitled, a frequent problem of public assistance recipients. An individual and an organization may be in conflict over the fate of someone for whom both have responsibility, as may occur between a parent and a school or a relative and a hospital. An inmate may feel he is being treated unfairly by an institution: the only problem a juvenile may acknowledge is his trouble with the court.

The client must of course perceive his difficulty in these terms, before it becomes a target problem. An organization's definition of an individual's problem, or the caseworker's judgment that he is not being adequately served by an agency, do not "give" the client a problem in his relations with a formal organization. The caseworker may try to help him see that he has such a problem, but that is a different matter.

On the other hand, a client may view his problem as one of this type, only to have his perceptions brushed aside by caseworkers more interested in psychological or interpersonal difficulties. Caseworkers attuned to the importance of such problems will be more likely to identify and accredit them.

DIFFICULTIES IN ROLE PERFORMANCE. If the client's major concern is his difficulty in carrying out a particular social role, then his problem falls in this category. Most problems of this type that caseworkers are apt to deal with concern family roles, usually roles of spouse or parent, although roles of student, employee, and patient also receive considerable emphasis in casework practice. Our use of the term "role" is limited to achieved roles, those the client has attained, rather than those ascribed to him because of his biological characteristics, such as his age or sex.

Clients with perceived problems in role performance are, by definition, aware of a gap between how they actually execute their roles and how they would like to. A mother may see herself as demanding too much of her children, a husband may acknowledge that he is too critical of his wife, a college student may be troubled by his inability to invest himself in his studies. In helping clients specify such problems, it is advisable to pin down in detail discrepancies between the client's real and desired behavior.

In problems of family relations, it may be hard sometimes to decide whether a difficulty is best classified as one of interpersonal conflict or one of role performance, since there may be elements of both types of problems. If two family members perceive a shared relational problem, interpersonal conflict would be the usual classification, since it is unlikely that each would view the problem as a deficiency in his own role behavior. The role performance category is used most often when only one member in a disturbed relation perceives a problem. Thus a mother may come to an agency full of complaints about her adolescent daughter with whom she is in obvious conflict over a variety of issues. The daughter may acknowledge no problem at all. To view the problem simply as interpersonal conflict might not provide the best direction for intervention if the daughter—"one half" of the conflict—proved to be inaccessible to help. It might be more strategic to attempt to help the mother identify what she might do to improve the situation. Hence aspects of her role performance might well emerge as the target problem, with due recognition of the limitations of this classification and despite the "objective" elements of conflict in the relationship.

PROBLEMS OF SOCIAL TRANSITION. Movement from one social position, role, or situation to another is a frequent source of problems of living. Events as apparently diverse as discharge from a hospital or institution, migration to a different locale, becoming a parent, or getting a divorce have in common one central theme: abrupt change in the individual's social field.

Two kinds of problems associated with social transitions are frequently dealt with by social workers. One concerns dilemmas about potential changes: whether an unwed, pregnant girl will keep or surrender her future child; whether a wife will leave her husband; whether a student will stay in school or leave to take a job; whether a family will remain in the community or seek its fortune elsewhere. The client is faced with a difficult choice, usually between maintaining his present position and change. His uncertainties about what course to pursue constitute the heart of this kind of problem.

The other kind of problem of social transition often encountered occurs after a change has been decided upon, as in the case of a patient ready for discharge, an older person who has chosen to enter a residential home, or a family that has decided to move. Caseworkers are familiar with the manifold problems that may arise in the course of such transitions: the client's lack of needed information and resources; his feelings of upset over the impending or actual change; and needs for complex planning and coordination often involving a number of individuals or organizations.

REACTIVE EMOTIONAL DISTRESS. Anxiety, depression, or other expressions of disturbed affective states are likely to accompany each of the problems that have been described thus far. A client experiencing interpersonal conflict or undergoing a difficult social transition can hardly be expected to remain unperturbed. Still the client who has such problems does not present the upset in his feelings as his primary concern. He may feel distressed about this relationship with his spouse but he wants help primarily with his marital difficulty and not his feelings about it.

In problems of reactive emotional distress, however, the client's major concern is with his feelings themselves rather than the situation that may have given rise to them. This may be so not only because of his distress but also because there may be little he can do about the precipitating events, either because they have already occurred or because they are beyond his control. In order to be classified in the present category, however, his distress must be reactive to a specific event or set of circumstances that can be readily identified, such as the death of a family member, loss of status, separation from a loved one, financial difficulties, or illness. If it is, then the problem meets our general criterion—that the problem be one the client is able to act on—since his knowledge of the cause enables him to take certain actions. Even if the precipitating event has already passed, he can gain relief from talking to others, from reflection, from working or, in the case of a loss, from searching for compensating sources of need-fulfillment. If the cause of his upset is still active, as in the case of illness, indebtedness, and the like, he can of course do more, including action that might modify the cause itself. The caseworker then focuses his attention on how he can facilitate and augment the client's efforts at reducing his distress.

INADEQUATE RESOURCES. Target problems in this category arise when the client lacks tangible or specific resources: that is, he is in need of money, housing, food, transportation, a job, and so on. Needs of this kind do not in themselves, however, make *target* problems in this model; they do only if the caseworker is in a position to help the client secure them through systematic effort. Problems of resource needs that are simply referred to another agency, as is often the case, do not "count" as target problems in our system of bookkeeping.

ADDITIONAL CRITERIA

Within these general categories fall the problems to which our model is addressed. In order for a problem to be considered appropriate, however, it must meet three additional requirements.

First, we require that the client himself explicitly acknowledge the problem and express a willingness to work on it. This does not necessarily mean the client needs to seek out case-work help for a well-defined problem. He may come at the insistence of others or may be sought out by the caseworker. Initially he may recognize no problems he wishes to solve. But we do require that very soon in the client-caseworker encounter the client recognize a problem of concern to him. A target problem must then be one the client himself perceives as a problem. It may not be one that a referring organization had in mind, nor one that the caseworker views as the most impor-tant, but it does represent, by definition, some difficulty that the client wishes to alleviate. In our judgment this quality alone makes the problem worthy of our full attention. It is from the problems as expressed by the client that the target problems are selected, with the greatest weight given to that problem of paramount concern to the client.

By taking this position we seek to avoid certain practices that we consider generally unrewarding for both caseworker and client. One such practice consists of fruitless efforts, sometimes extending over months, to engage semi-captive clients in helping relationships that they have not asked for, do not want, and probably cannot use.

Another practice we wish to avoid is what we refer to as "double agenda" casework. The client may indeed acknowl-edge a problem that he wants help with, but the caseworker and agency see him as having other problems, usually of a graver sort, that are more deserving of attention. Thus the problem of concern to the client does not become the target of intervention; the target, rather, becomes some underlying dif-ficulty that the client is not aware he has or at any rate has not asked for help with. The client pursues his agenda, which may call for obtaining a needed resource or securing help with an immediate problem, while the caseworker doggedly pursues a different agenda, namely one of trying to get the client to see the "real" problem underneath it all.

For example, a mother is referred to a social agency by a school because family problems are interfering with her son's scholastic performance. While perhaps admitting to some domestic difficulties, the mother does not recognize any meaningful connection between them and her son's school performance. She rather sees his difficulty as due primarily to the school's mishandling. While the caseworker sees "some reality" to the mother's complaint about the school, he also sees vast vistas of family pathology. The caseworker is apt to show little interest in the former, while pursuing the latter with vigor. Reluctance on the client's part to join the pursuit becomes labeled as resistance or denial. Our approach would suggest that the emphasis be reversed in this case. Once having explored the family situation with the mother and having determined any lack of a perceived problem on her part, the caseworker would then turn his attention to the mother's problem in relation with a formal organization, namely the school; and intervention would be confined to helping her with this difficulty.

A second requirement for a target problem in our model is this: the client should be in a position to take action to alleviate the problem, with the caseworker serving as his agent in this task. This requirement asks that the problem to be dealt with falls within the scope of the combined resources of the client and caseworker. Otherwise there is nothing to hit the target with. Very often clients present caseworkers with problems that fail to meet this requirement, and very often caseworkers seem to act as if they accept such problem definitions.

For example, in problems of family relations there is a general tendency for clients to define problems primarily as difficulties in the behavior of other family members rather than as problems in their own behavior. A wife may view the main problem as her husband's impossible behavior, with the husband's view just the opposite. As long as the clients define their problem in these terms, there is little basis for constructive action on the part of either client since each regards the necessary action as coming from the other. If the caseworker gives tacit acceptance to these definitions by not challenging them, then he is trapped in a hopeless double agent role. What can he do with either client if each is waiting expectantly for the other to act? No target problem has yet been defined. Although an observer might view the couple as having an obvious problem of interpersonal conflict, the partners themselves see the problem as inadequate role performance on the part of each other and the solution as lying in the action of the other.

A common strategy in long-term treatment is to accept passively such definitions until a "relationship is established," then eventually to try to help the client understand his own contribution to the problem and to discover ways of acting differently. There is not time available in short-term work for such a gradual approach and, in our view, this is just as well since we think it is counter-productive in any case. Until an appropriate target problem has been defined with the client in such situations, there is little basis for meaningful client-worker communication. Moreover the caseworker's tacit acceptance of the client's view that the problem resides exclusively in another person may serve to reinforce this view, making the job of changing it all the more difficult later on. We suggest that the caseworker and the client identify a problem that the client can act on at the beginning of contact, usually no later than the second interview, and not to proceed further until such a problem is identified.

What we have said in respect to the second requirement in no way contradicts our position that the caseworker should give priority to the target problem as perceived by the client. The second requirement arises only when the client, in fact, does not perceive a problem that constitutes an appropriate target of intervention. Both requirements add up to asking the caseworker to address his efforts to a problem the client both wants to work on and is able to work on.

If the caseworker and client cannot identify any problem meeting these two requirements in the initial phase, then as a general rule we see little basis to continue with any form of casework treatment. If the client has been given the opportunity to explore and assess potential problems in his life situation and to learn of the kind of help the caseworker may be able to give, he should then be in a position to make a rational decision about his need for casework. If his decision is negative, it should be respected. By so doing we attest to the client's right to make such a decision, and at the same time we accept the reality that we can probably not accomplish much in any case with a client who does not want help. But as we see it, this rule is general rather than absolute, and exceptions, some of which will be noted in other contexts, are certainly possible.

Our third requirement is that the problem be relatively limited and specific in nature, an essential criterion in short-term models, and we would suggest, a desirable one for casework practice in general. But such a standard is meaningless unless it can be defined, and this is difficult to do on an abstract level. Perhaps we can convey an impression of our conception of problem scope by considering two types of problems that are likely to be defined in rather global terms. We are referring to problems of interpersonal conflict and role performance. Definitions on the order of "a breakdown in communication between husband and wife" or "inadequacies in carrying out the maternal role" are too global to be acceptable in our system. We ask that problems of interpersonal conflict be specified in terms of particular issues around which conflict occurs, and problems of role performance be specified in terms of the particular aspects of the role that is affected. Thus a target problem might concern conflict between husband and wife over the disciplining of their son or the inability of a mother to provide adequate physical care for her sixteen-month-old infant. We are not asking simply for a certain way of recording problems; rather, we are asking that the targets of intervention themselves be sharply limited.

It may seem to some that we are being overly restrictive, if not precious, in our insistence that the target problem be one that the client expresses a willingness to work on, can do something about with the help of the caseworker, and that is limited in scope. We would say, rather, that these requirements reflect the limitations of casework as an agent of change. We assume that casework may be effective with problems so defined, though we have no incontrovertible evidence that this is so. If one wishes to assume a broader range of effectiveness for casework, then the burden of proof is greater, we think. There is certainly little evidence, for example, to suggest that casework can bring about significant change with clients who do *not* express a clear desire to work on problems that the caseworker wishes to pursue. If casework has such a capability, one would expect it to emerge in studies in which casework service is offered to clients without self-perceived problems they expressly wish to work on. Experimental tests of this casework approach have failed to demonstrate its efficacy (Meyer, Borgatta, and Jones, 1965; Wallace, 1967; Mullen, Chazin, and Feldstein, 1970).

While we think that the problem typology comprises most of the problems caseworkers can be expected to deal with successfully, it is not meant to be exhaustive. It certainly does not span the range of human problems that caseworkers currently deal with. Nor does it necessarily exhaust the totality of problems that may be amenable to the kind of brief treatment design presented in this book. These are the problem types thus far *identified* as appropriate for our model.

There is little to be gained from commenting extensively on problems to which the model is *not* addressed, since the concerns already identified are more than enough to occupy us. We shall give, however, some of our reasons for excluding certain kinds of problems that caseworkers sometimes treat.

A range of problems were ruled out because we would not expect them to respond to short-term casework methods. Well-established personality and behavior disorders fall here. Our model is not designed to treat neurosis, character disorders, alcoholism, drug addiction, and the like. We also question, as do most caseworkers, whether any form of casework, no matter how extended, can accomplish much with problems of this type. Certain problems which are considered appropriate targets in some short-term models were excluded because, as yet, we are not sure how our approach might be applied to them. For the most part these are problems in which it is not clear what remedial action the client might take; hence it becomes difficult to identify potential tasks. Emotional reactions with unknown origins, psychogenic conditions, and habit disorders are examples. Although in a subsequent chapter, we consider possible adaptations of the model to direct work with children, we should note here that the target problems we have presented, as well as the model as a whole, have been designed for direct work with adults and adolescents, and not children.

What may first appear to be a difficulty not falling within our typology may turn out to fit into one of our categories. Initial complaints of inexplicable anxiety, depression, and the like may, on closer inspection, turn out to have social origins which the client may volunteer himself or readily acknowledge when pointed out to him. Such complaints may emerge as less important to the client than a problem in his social network that he wishes help with. At a more general level, it is important to keep in mind that exclusion of certain problems does not mean that individuals who happen to have these problems cannot be treated for other problems they may possess. A client who may be psychotic, alcoholic, and phobic may want help for problems included in our typology. Such help, quite possibly, can be given while he is receiving other forms of treatment elsewhere for his other difficulties. Finally, practitioners are free to adapt our treatment approach to whatever kinds of problems might in their judgment benefit from it, whether or not the problems can be fitted into our scheme. The current domain of the model, defined by the problem categories that have been identified, is certainly open to expansion.

PROBLEM EXPLORATION

The practitioner's first step in applying the present model is to explore the problems the client may wish help for. The caseworker's attention is concentrated on what the client perceives as perplexities in his current life situation, regardless of how his problems may be defined by persons or organizations in his social network. Often, the client's problem is initially defined for the social worker by someone other than the client himself—a family member, a physician, teacher, and the like. These conceptions of the problem may be considered important elements in the client's social network and, as such, are to be taken into account in problem exploration. They do not, however, determine its ultimate focus. In the course of his exploration the caseworker may, in effect, ask the client if he shares the view of some problem-definer or determine the client's opinion of this view. The caseworker may even present a case for the validity of someone else's conception of the problem. But all of this is secondary to an exploration of what the client perceives his difficulties to be, since the target problem must be one the client himself wishes to resolve.

Often there are two levels which have to be explored in specifying the characteristics of the problem as perceived by the client. The client's initial expression of the problem, usually at the beginning of the first interview, may be colored by pent-up affect, by his discomfort over talking to a stranger, or by his uncertainties about the kind of help that will be offered. At this "first level" of expression, the client may not reveal the problem about which he is most concerned. As the interview proceeds the client, helped along by the caseworker's inquiries and explanations, usually reaches the point where he can start to express the difficulties that are troubling him the most. It is at this "second level" that potential target problems begin to emerge. Given the narrowness of focus on the "here and now," the quality of specificity that is being sought should be achieved either at some point in the initial interview (of 1 to 1½ hours duration) or in the second interview. This process can be observed in the following illustration:

Mrs. Small, a forty-five-year-old black woman, widowed and a welfare recipient, was referred to a medical social service department by a physician for exploration of various social stresses which seemed to be aggravating her physical complaints. Her demeanor revealed obvious upset which she attributed to her worry about a teenage girl for whom she had charge and who was living with her. The girl was pregnant for the second time and was unmarried. This woman perceived her problem as needing to do "something" about her ward and being unsure about what should be done, although she concentrated on the possibility of placing this girl somewhere outside of her own home.

The second interview, which was held in the home and which included the teenager, revealed that Mrs. Small had been awarded custody of the girl by the juvenile court, that the girl was her niece. Except for a brief time, Mrs. Small had reared the girl since infancy. Mrs. Small was feeling pressure from a hostile court probation officer to place the girl in a state school for delinquents, as punishment for her sexual transgressions. These pressures reinforced Mrs. Small's ambivalence about her ward. But Mrs. Small was also immensely fond of the girl and altruistically concerned about her future.

However, these two, who lived together in close family intimacy, never talked together about these problems.

The perceived problem emerged not as Mrs. Small's confusion about where the young girl should be placed, but how these two women could understand enough about one another and the problem of the pregnancy so that they could plan co-operatively.

The target problem may not be expressed at the first level, since the client's initially unexpressed concerns may be the ones he most wants help with. When the client is certain at the outset of the problem he wishes to work on, he may never reach the second level. The notion of two levels of problem expression still applies to a large number of cases in which there is a distinction between the problem the client initially presents and the one he wants help with.

DETERMINING THE TARGET PROBLEM

In his initial exploration of the client's problem situation, the caseworker is likely to locate several problems that the client might want help with. It has proved possible in the clinical trials of this model to use a reasonably systematic method for "zeroing in" on the major target problem. This process can be schematized thus:

1. *The array of problems with which the client appears now to be concerned is elicited.*

2. *The different problems or different aspects of problems are defined in explicit behavioral terms.*

3. *The problems are ranked into an order of priority according to where the major emphasis is placed by the client.*

Some clients may be able to do their own ranking according to their own priorities. In other cases, a ranking is inferred from certain observable behavior, such as the amount of distress the client expresses when he discusses a problem. The caseworker's inferred ranking is then checked out with the client.

4. *The target problem is tentatively determined in collaboration with the client.*

The problem the client is most interested in resolving is normally the one selected, assuming it is one that the caseworker and client together have the resources to resolve or alleviate. In some cases more than one target problem is selected, particularly if the problems are interrelated.

5. *The target problem is classified by the caseworker.*

Classifying the problem means deciding into which of the various problem categories the difficulty most logically falls. As has been noted, these problem categories are not precisely defined. In order to use such a rough typology to best advantage, it is usually necessary for the practitioner to make arbitrary judgments. He must place a problem into that classification which most nearly represents the major problem in living perceived now by the client. Such a perception may be different in whole or in part from the perception of significant others, including the practitioner. To proceed systematically with this model, however, such a judgment appears to be essential because, as will emerge later, the problem classification will establish the boundaries of the assessment and will guide task selection and treatment strategy.

6. *The target problem is specified through further exploration.*

The particular characteristics of the problem are delineated and, if necessary, the scope of the problem is narrowed to bring it within manageable limits.

Two examples will illustrate these processes:

Mrs. E * was a hospital in-patient being treated for a severe liver disease. Because she was showing high anxiety, and because her chronic alcoholism was considered to be the cause of her illness, she was referred to the hospital social service department. The implied expectation of the medical staff was that social service might contain the destructive drinking problem.

The first interview revealed a forty-year-old black woman, unmarried, a public assistance recipient. Her eighteen-year-old severely mentally retarded daughter had always lived at home with her. The daughter was temporarily with the maternal grandparents during Mrs. E's hospitalization.

Mrs. E's first level description of her overriding concerns was the inadequacy of her welfare payments. She gave information about this difficulty at length, accompanied by intense anger and anxiety. After this she tearfully related her concerns over the future care of her daughter and her wish to keep the daughter at home, where she would be lovingly attended. Her deep emotional involvement with her daughter became apparent. Her recital about her daughter used less time than her communications about her financial difficulties, but was ex-

---

* Mrs. E and other illustrative cases identified by an alphabetic code were drawn from the caseload of one of the projects reported in chapter 11. Outcome data for each of these cases is presented in Table 1 on pages 234–35.

pressed with greater feeling. Next, she said angrily she had been deprived all her life by her harsh mother who openly preferred her siblings to herself. Then Mrs. E commented upon her awareness that she might die from her present illness. This was offered quietly and factually and tied to concerns that her daughter should be well cared for. As soon as she again mentioned her daughter the affect rose. Last, Mrs. E spoke of her awareness that her long-standing drinking problem had vastly complicated her existence, and she pronounced a resolve never to drink again when she got out of the hospital.

The array of problems approximately in the order revealed by Mrs. E is presented below:

1. Clothes and food needs   First level of expression
2. Daughter's care
3. Deprived relationships, especially past   Second level of expression
4. Fear of dying
5. Drinking

Because of the high quantity and critical quality of the client's affect concerning her daughter, the practitioner ranked the problem of the daughter's care first. The client confirmed the practitioner's judgment. The problem was classified as one of *role performance,* specified as mother's need to develop ways of caring for her daughter more properly at home.

Mrs. Murphy, thirty years old, white, lower middle class, was referred to a mental health clinic by her private physician. He was concerned about the extent of her apparent depressive reaction to the news that she was suffering from a gynecological disease and would need to be treated for a protracted time. While painful, the condition was curable and not incapacitating. Hence, the quantity of her depression seemed excessive. During her initial interview at the clinic, Mrs. Murphy talked first of her depression about the medical diagnosis, having been thoroughly prepared by her physician to do so and because the caseworker opened the interview on this focus. It emerged during this interview that her feelings of depression were related not primarily to her medical condition but to conflict with her husband and her employer, both of whom were angry about her excessive drinking. She was feeling threatened with the possible loss of her husband's love and was torn by the strains in her marital and work relationships.

Mrs. Murphy's concerns, in the order in which they emerged in the interview were as follows:

1. Depression over illness   First level expression of problem
2. Excessive drinking   ⎫
3. Conflicts related to   ⎬ Second level expression
   marriage and job   ⎭ of problem

The problem might have been specified as her drinking to excess, or as her distress over her illness or over her estrangement from her husband. Since the patient's pervasive emphasis in her recital was upon the conflict she was experiencing with her husband, her major target problem was defined as interpersonal conflict. A second target problem—role performance at work—was also identified.

As this case illustrates, it is possible to deal with more than one kind of target problem in task-centered casework, although in our experience with the model there have been few cases in which more than two different types of target problems have been addressed. It seems in most cases that the client's major concerns do not span more than two categories of the problem typology and are usually centered in one. Normally, then, the bulk of the caseworker's and the client's attention is given to one problem system. While more than one target problem may be identified within a category—thus a married couple may have more than one problem of interpersonal conflict—the usual tendency is to deal with one focal problem within each category.

In some cases, however, the caseworker is presented with a formidable variety of problems. The client may want help with several problems; or more likely is unable to focus his request in a way that would give the caseworker a sense of direction. Perhaps the most challenging case of this kind is the family with a mixture of relational difficulties and resource inadequacies, problems which may affect several family members. Such cases are fewer in number than might be supposed when we consider that such families, despite a multiplicity of problems, often want the caseworker's help around some particular need or issue. Still some families present an array of problems that would "overload" the capabilities of any brief treatment design. We are not sure at this point how such families can best be served within the limits of the model, or how the model can be modified to help them.

It is possible that several different problems could be addressed, with concentration on the more critical. The target problems would need to be limited in scope and, if at all possible, to be interrelated in order to avoid a dispersal of effort which would parallel the dispersal of problems.

The use of teams of practitioners may be a means of helping individuals or families with a variety of problems within the limits of short-term treatment. The service design utilized by Schwartz and Sample (1966), in which graduate caseworkers supervised teams of assistants who were assigned specific responsibilities on specific cases, was an apparently more effective method of helping families receiving public assistance than the conventional arrangement of having a single caseworker totally responsible for a family's service needs. Adapting the Schwartz-Sample design to our model, a caseworker and one or more assistants might work with a family toward the achievement of multiple tasks, with different tasks the responsibility of different team members. Carol Meyer (1970) has described a number of ways in which "professional-technical social work teams" are, or could be, organized (pp. 213–20). Her framework offers a basis for the development of several variations of brief task-centered casework in which teams, rather than individual practitioners, might be utilized in work with clients who want help with a range of problems.

PERSONS WHO DO NOT
ACKNOWLEDGE PROBLEMS

Many individuals and families who come to caseworkers, or whom caseworkers are asked to see, express no problems they want the caseworkers' help with. Parents may come to a family agency on the urging of a school psychologist who is of the opinion that their child is underachieving because of family problems, but the parents (who dutifully report to the agency to appease the school) see their child as "just lazy"—nothing at home could be contributing to his poor performance. A teenage girl, pregnant out-of-wedlock, is referred to a case-worker for planning regarding her unborn child but turns out to have made up her mind to keep the baby and does not want the caseworker's counsel, except for some advice about medical arrangements. A young man brought to a hospital emergency room because of a suicide attempt tells the case-worker that he prefers to work out his problem on his own.

In the present model the caseworker has an obligation to inform the would-be client of the kind of help he is equipped and prepared to give. This should be done in a straightfor-ward way, at the beginning of contact. If the person referred sees nothing in the caseworker's offering that would be of any use to him, the caseworker may suggest that it might be worthwhile for both of them to consider whether or not there is a problem the caseworker might be able to be of help with. Such a "problem-search" should be undertaken only if the client agrees to it and understands what it entails. The search should be time-limited—generally not exceeding two inter-views—and the limits should be made clear. It should be understood that if no problem is located within whatever number of interviews is agreed upon, the caseworker will go no further. If the person referred rejects the offer of an explo-ration of his situation, then the contact should not be pro-longed much beyond that point, except in those cases in which the caseworker is charged with a clear "protective" function (see chapter 10).

The C case illustrates a successful problem search. Mrs. C had undergone surgery on her right hand for removal of a growth caused by thirty years of working in her own beauty shop, shampooing hair. The left hand was also affected and would need surgery after the right hand was healed. She would be unable to work at her occupation for months, per-haps never again. Mrs. C was white, middle-middle class, and aged fifty-five. Her husband, aged sixty, had suffered his sec-ond heart attack six months before her surgery, was unem-ployed and receiving $185 per month disability benefits. He had been a foreman in a machine shop and could never again work except at hard-to-find sedentary jobs for which he had no training. She was referred to the social service department of a clinic because she seemed depressed.

In the first interview she was told of the reason for the re-ferral. Although depressed, she was in control of her feelings and she said there was nothing at all she wanted or needed. Since it appeared most likely that this couple was undergoing massive stress and it was not at all clear how they could sup-port themselves financially, it was suggested that another talk together might be useful to see if there was an area which could be worked on. With some reluctance Mrs. C agreed to a home visit. Her reluctance was so strong that no more than one interview was proposed.

The visit revealed that Mr. and Mrs. C lived in the rear of her beauty shop, now unused and deserted, in a building owned by her aged father who lived upstairs. After some pre-liminaries, they were asked what their plans were. Mr. C could say little. He was physically better now but he could never expect to return to work. Mrs. C was thinking of open-ing her shop again and shampooing no matter what excruciat-ing pain she felt and no matter what the consequences. Both seemed to be blocking out the seriousness of their situation, before which they were helpless.

The caseworker said that she hoped the couple would not misunderstand her intrusiveness but she failed to see how

Mrs. C could shampoo hair with her hand in a cast and the other one soon to be in the same condition. Since the medical prognosis was guarded, the caseworker could not have much confidence that Mrs. C could depend on her hands enough to keep her at her employment. She added that she also failed to understand how Mr. C could be satisfied simply sitting and looking out the shop window while his wife painfully washed hair for customers who would soon not come back with such conditions in the shop.

The gloom which descended at this point was immense. After saying she was sorry to cause them distress, the practitioner asked the couple if she was perhaps overstating the case. No, she was not, they said. The caseworker then asked them how they were managing financially. Could they get along on what was coming in from benefits? Yes, they could get along meagerly, and they supposed they would have to. However, after long years of labor and struggle, during which they reared two children successfully, they were appalled at the prospect of being helpless and useless before they were even very old. Here their depression became evident and they ruminated upon it for some time. They saw no way out.

The practitioner stated that she would not underestimate the difficulties, and she did not think that things would ever again be as they had been; but she said she saw both as capable persons with an ability to do something about their situation if they would not permit themselves to be overwhelmed. Now Mr. and Mrs. C wanted to know what she saw in them, so she ticked off what she had observed and inferred to be strengths—their capacity for hard work, their resourcefulness. Both of them then acknowledged that perhaps they needed to find a way to do something, perhaps some kind of work or activities, until perhaps Mrs. C could resume her regular occupation. Thus it was possible to locate a target problem, classified as one of *social transition*.

This case also illustrates the use of diagnostic hypotheses (a subject dealt with more extensively at a later point) in helping clients locate problems. The caseworker's explorations were guided by the hypothesis that Mr. and Mrs. C's depressive reactions resulted in large part from their loss of occupational roles. Although there were obviously other causes of their depression, such as their physical ailments, the loss of occupational roles was seen as a "manipulable cause," one the caseworker and the clients could do something about and hence one of particular importance.

Not all such efforts to locate problems are successful, as the following case illustrates:

Mrs. Dale is a black, forty-four-year-old widow, the mother of eleven children, and a welfare recipient. She came to a medical clinic with complaints of dizziness and fatigue. The medical finding was moderate hypertension which did not yield to medication. She was referred to the social service department for exploration of social and interpersonal problems which might account for her tensions.

The first interview revealed many apparent problems. Chronic severe impoverishment pervaded Mrs. Dale's life. Her whole existence consisted of housework and child care. There was no evidence that her children were in trouble and no evidence of serious parent-child problems. Although her two eldest were grown and out of the home, the remaining nine required burdensome physical labor and almost all her attention. She had not dated during her widowhood of seven years and seemed to have relinquished all interest in male companions.

It was explained that she had been asked to see the social worker because it was a common finding among hypertensive people that personal and family stresses could defeat medical treatment. She found this explanation perfectly sensible and offered, at once, her own prescription for relief from the family burdens she described. She would like to take a vacation trip to another city where she had relatives and where she fantasied she might rest. There were no resources available for carrying out such a plan. There was nothing she could suggest that she might do, other than going away for a while, which would relieve her of her sense of being overburdened or her conviction that she must keep on doggedly doing everything that she was doing.

The immediate offer of a homemaker to give her a bit of a vacation at home was rejected out-of-hand as being more trouble than it was worth. All efforts to discuss with her things she could do to alleviate her onerous pattern met with a blank wall. Two more interviews were held with the explicit objective of pursuing the problem search further. While these interviews revealed additional areas of difficulty in Mrs. Dale's life, there emerged no problems that she wanted to work on with the caseworker. Thus, contact ended at the completion of the problem exploration phase, three interviews in this case.

This example is typical of general casework practice in certain respects. The caseworker attempted to help the client locate a problem the client might have wanted help with but did not succeed. Nonetheless it illustrates certain distinctive features of task-centered casework. The problem-search was carried out with a mutual understanding of its purpose, nature, and limits. The client was not asked to keep appointments simply because she seemed to have problems that the caseworker could help her with or because the doctor thought she should. When casework is an adjunct to some service which the client needs, medical care in this case, it is possible for caseworkers to see semi-captive clients in lengthy but unproductive relationships around vaguely defined problems that the client does not want help for and, hence, cannot be helped with. This was not done in the case of Mrs. Dale.

But what of the presumed psychogenetic factors contributing to Mrs. Dale's medical condition? Undoubtedly her personality structure, life style, and current problems of living aggravated her physical problems. Knowledge of this kind, however, does not necessarily give us the means to help such a client through casework or other forms of interpersonal treatment. Obviously such means are not provided by the present model and we know of no other casework model in which they are.

The practitioner still has a responsibility, of course, to help clients whom he cannot treat adequately himself to make use of other forms of treatment that may be helpful. In the case of Mrs. Dale this did not prove to be possible, but certainly there would be many clients who might not be able to utilize task-centered casework but who might be helped in one way or another by quite different methods such as long-term psychotherapy, group treatment, chemotherapy, and behavior modification.

Mrs. Dale was an articulate, intelligent, and thoughtful woman who was candid with the social worker. She was aware of all her problems and she believed that the stresses in her life could be reinforcing her illness. At the level of her self-awareness, she did not want or need to be sick, or a martyr. The speculation that her independence was to a great extent false and that she had enormous disguised dependency needs has merit, particularly in view of what is commonly understood about the underlying emotional features of her disease. Nevertheless, Mrs. Dale was immune to this kind of insight and uninterested in the topic. She thought of life problems as being pressures stemming from events produced in her environment. If such events were to become too burdensome, she might want to get help from social workers or any other source which could offer her tangible resources. But otherwise, she viewed herself as thoroughly competent about how to conduct her affairs.

Treatment of Mrs. Dale's possible psychological problems was clearly an impossibility since she was unmotivated and would not consent or submit. This case illustrates, however, a dilemma for social workers, many of whom are dependent upon referral sources and have a commitment to collaboration with other professionals (in this instance with a physician) who may have higher status.

Some caseworkers seem to persist with unwilling clients in unproductive relationships out of a sense of obligation to the referral source or, perhaps, to avoid the criticism that they are unwilling to extend themselves with difficult clients. Such persistence is misplaced, in our judgment. Casework's referral sources and supporting public perhaps understand better than many caseworkers that little can be achieved with clients who fundamentally do not want help.

Other professionals or community members who expect the caseworker to "help" the unwilling client perhaps need to understand the limitations of his position and his art, and the best person to explain these limitations is the caseworker himself. Suppose, for example, a medical social worker refers a patient with a physical deformity to a physician for possible corrective surgery. The person sees the physician, is informed of what can be done, is advised of the possible benefits, but still refuses treatment. The doctor does not feel he has failed to live up to his obligations nor do we hold him responsible for the patient's refusal to cooperate. The same logic should apply when a doctor refers a patient to a medical social worker for a social problem. In our efforts to justify casework services we have often blurred critical distinctions between what we can reasonably expect to accomplish and what would be desirable to accomplish. Such distinctions, we think, need to be more sharply drawn.

REACHING AGREEMENT
ON THE TARGET PROBLEM

Normally the process of defining and ranking problems will provide clarity about the focus of work. The caseworker should make sure, however, that he and the client are in accord on the target problems. This step is critical in situations in which possible target problems are numerous or complex.

An explicit agreement between the caseworker and client is called for. Usually the caseworker states the substance of what he and the client have apparently agreed upon, and then asks if this formulation adequately reflects the client's understanding of the problems to be dealt with. If more than one problem is to be worked on, then it should be made clear which, if any, is to be given the greatest emphasis and which, if any, is to be taken up first. Any misunderstandings between the client and caseworker that are brought to light should be discussed forthwith. While the participants need to be in substantial agreement on at least one problem before further work can proceed, there may be certain areas of disagreement or uncertainty that can not be resolved at this juncture. These areas should be clarified. Thus the caseworker and client may agree that major attention will be given to her son's problems with his teacher; they may further agree that the client's own problems with her son may be dealt with later on, if the client (who has doubts that such problems exist) decides she wants to work on them.

ANALYSIS OF THE PROBLEM

In order to develop a strategy for dealing with a problem, it is helpful to have some understanding of what is producing it. Analysis of the problem is addressed to locating its immediate causes as a basis for selection of the task. As a step in the model, problem analysis occurs following agreement upon target problems, although normally a good part of the analysis takes place during problem exploration. Problem analysis is a joint undertaking of caseworker and client, usually guided by the caseworker's inquiries. The amount of analysis necessary or possible in the initial phase depends entirely on the target problem. Explorations for some problems are soon apparent: a man cannot find a job because of lack of marketable work skills or a woman is depressed because her husband, on whom she is strongly dependent, has left her. More complex problems require more extended analysis. A couple that quarrels incessantly over "in-law" relationships may present a problem that demands fairly extensive inquiry about the perceptions and motivations of each as well as their relationships with their extended families. With any problem, particularly the more complex, only so much can be accomplished in portions of one or two interviews. The process of problem analysis is continued as a part of subsequent steps of the model. As will be seen, work on the task, particularly helping the client to overcome obstacles to task achievement, necessarily involves further analysis of the problem.

But in the initial phase efforts to understand the problem are carried only as far as necessary to establish what action, in general, the client can take to alleviate it. The plan of action may need to be revised in the light of further insight into the problems, but that is no reason for not helping the client shape his problem reducing efforts. In most cases these efforts are already underway before the caseworker makes his appearance, and they will be continued regardless of the amount of understanding of the problem the caseworker or the client possess.

While a comprehension of what is causing the problem may be desirable as a basis for corrective action, we subscribe to Briar and Miller's position (1971) that "not only have effective treatment strategies been developed in the absence of knowledge about cause, but knowledge of cause may not be sufficient, or even in some instances useful, in devising intervention measures" (p. 154). Perhaps such understanding becomes necessary only if one assumes that the practitioner holds the key to the solution. Then he must "diagnose" before he can treat; otherwise he would not know which key to use. But if one assumes, as we do, that the solution lies primarily in the action the client is willing and able to take, then our perspective is altered. Problem-solving models of behavior notwithstanding, people can and do take effective action to resolve their problems without much apparent comprehension of their causes, and often without much thought about them. The failing student one day decides to "get down to work" and does, without realizing that the reason for his poor performance, perhaps, lay in "his fears of success." Similarly, a couple may get a divorce, certainly one solution to a marital problem, without knowing why their marriage failed.

THE PRACTITIONER'S
DIAGNOSTIC JUDGMENTS

In our preceding discussion of the target problem we merged two quite distinct aspects of the caseworker's role: one is the caseworker's communications with the client in the process of exploring, identifying, and analyzing target problems; the other is the caseworker's cognitive operations—what goes on inside his head as he tries to make sense out of the data he is receiving about the client's problems. As he talks and listens, the practitioner is constantly engaged in making diagnostic judgments about the client and his problem. These judgments, which are a joint product of the information he has gathered about the case and his professional knowledge, are important since they largely determine what the practitioner does at a given point in a given case.

In the present model, the practitioner's judgments are first addressed to questions concerning the client's problems: How can his target problem best be classified and specified? How can it best be explained? His diagnostic thinking is problem-oriented in two senses. First, his data base consists primarily of information he has received in the course of his exploration and analysis of the client's problem. Second, his judgments themselves are concerned mainly with definition and explanation of the problem rather than with the client's personality or situation in any comprehensive way.

Diagnostic judgments in task-centered casework evolve incrementally from the continuous flow of information the caseworker receives as he carries out the steps of the model. There is no formal diagnostic phase, although the caseworker may be asked to record his diagnostic judgments at various points for administrative, teaching, or research purposes. While his operations depend on the information he receives and his assessment of it, the converse is also true: his diagnostic thinking is guided by the direction of his activity. If a decision is made to focus on a certain problem, then this decision becomes a determinant of subsequent diagnostic work. Thus diagnosis does not necessarily precede treatment; rather, the practitioner's diagnostic and treatment operations proceed in reciprocal fashion, each being a source of feedback for the other.

The caseworker's diagnostic efforts are set in motion when he first encounters a case and continue at a steady level as the case proceeds. They serve different functions at different steps, however. They are first addressed to problem definition and exploration; subsequently, as we shall see, they guide the practitioner's contribution to task selection and implementation.

As previously illustrated, these judgments may be organized into diagnostic hypotheses. In phases of work concerned with problem exploration and identification, these hypotheses are concerned with what problems the client may be perceiving, which of these problems are most important to him, what factors are contributing to them, and so on. Like any hypothesis, a diagnostic hypothesis is a statement to be tested. It may be descriptive ("Mrs. Green seems to be mostly concerned about her relationship with her husband") or explanatory ("Mr. White's fears of being rejected seem to be one reason why he is reluctant to apply for the job"). The hypotheses are tested and revised through data obtained from the client or others. Strong weight is given phenomenological data supplied by the client, in other words, the client's expressions about himself and his world. Thus in the examples above, the caseworker might test his hypotheses by asking Mrs. Brown about the importance of her problem with her husband and Mr. White about his fears of being rejected. Essentially negative responses from the clients (assuming their responses were adequately probed) would cast doubt on the usefulness of the hypotheses, if not their validity. In either case the client might be withholding his true feelings or might be unaware of them; but there would then be the question of how the caseworker might test these new hypotheses, given the limitations of his data.

Even if he were able to build an inferential case that the clients were reacting in ways contrary to their own account of their behavior, he would have to ask himself how such hypotheses could be put to use in helping the client define his problems and determine ways of solving them. Above all else, diagnostic hypotheses in this model should serve the pragmatic function of helping the client move ahead with his problem-solving tasks. If the caseworker's hypotheses make little sense to a client, the caseworker is well advised to formulate other hypotheses that the client can validate through his own statements and can assimilate in his own thinking.

CHAPTER FOUR

DURATION OF CASEWORK

AND PROBLEM-CHANGE

IN THIS chapter we present our rationale for the use of brief, task-centered casework treatment as a first choice treatment for the broad range of problems that comprise our domain. Our arguments can be used, we think, more generally to support large-scale use of planned brief treatment approaches, regardless of the particular form they take.

CHARACTERISTICS OF PROBLEM-CHANGE

A search for a theoretical ground for planned brevity might well begin with the question: How long does it take to achieve the kind of changes that are generally possible through casework? Obviously the answer depends on what we conceive our targets to be. If our target is a personality disorder, treatment is obviously going to take much longer than if our target is some specific behavior. The essence of our position is that the client himself has the primary responsibility for identifying the problem to be treated. In this view, therapeutic attention is addressed not to hypothetical disorders that we define but rather to what the client is complaining about and presumably wants help with. Thus our change efforts are directed at manifest problems of interpersonal conflict, role performance, and the like, rather than at underlying conditions as defined by the clinician. This does not mean that our diagnosis needs to be limited to the problems expressed by the client, that we should not address ourselves to the underlying causes of these problems in treatment, or that we do not have a responsibility to help clients recognize and express problems of which they are not immediately aware or that they cannot verbalize. It means rather that our definition of what we want to change should correspond closely to the client's initial or emergent conception of what he wants changed. The main rationale for this position is simply that the client will not let us do much else anyway—his conception of what he wants altered places stringent limits upon our helping efforts, no matter how well justified these may be in our value and theoretical systems.

If our targets are certain kinds of psychoscocial problems, then the change processes that characterize these problems must be taken into account in therapeutic efforts to alleviate them. That is, our attention is directed to a theory of problem-change rather than to theories of change in personality, attitudes, or behavior as such, even though such theories are germane to problem-change.

The way in which the targets of therapeutic intervention have been defined in our system serves as a basis for some formulations about how problems change, either with or without the help of professionals. We propose that change in such problems has three important characteristics: first, these problems are more likely to undergo change than to remain static; second, change is likely to be in the direction of problem reduction; third, the span of time in which most change is likely to occur is relatively brief, generally not more than a few months.

At a theoretical level these characteristics may be considered reflections of the systemic properties of the human behavior and social environments from which the problems emerge. The individual who acknowledges a problem is in a state of disequilibrium, which leads him to take action to resolve it. This push toward action is a critical feature of the homeostatic mechanisms that are called into play when problems arise. Since our concern is with those problems that the individual is willing to solve, the willingness itself is evidence that he is ready to take corrective action. Since his action is in the direction of problem reduction and since there are usually forces in his environment directed to the same purpose, most problems do become alleviated—that is, to the point that equilibrium is again achieved, and we think this happens soon. When it does, his own push for change is reduced, since it has accomplished its purpose. Often the restored equilibrium is a well-established problem state—a chronically conflicted interpersonal relationship, for example, that he has learned to live with; but once his problems have assumed their familiar shape, his drive for change diminishes.

We are suggesting a broader application of systems theory to problem-change than one finds in crisis theory (Rapoport, 1970). We have no quarrel with crisis theory, except that it seems to require that a person's equilibrium be upset by some identifiable hazardous event that precipitates a pronounced, if temporary, degree of disturbance in the individual. Such crises would make up, of course, a share of the problems to which we are referring.

But as we know, many of the problems clients bring to social agencies are chronic in nature. Difficulties in family relations, for example, usually fall into this category. While he is normally troubled, the client with a long-standing problem often does not appear to be in the throes of a crisis. In fact, it is often difficult to determine what exactly precipitated his decision to seek help. It is hard to fit such a case—and their numbers are legion—into crisis theory, as it is typically presented. We would suggest that a client who comes for help with a long-standing problem has usually experienced some breakdown, perhaps subtle, in his problem-managing capacity. His motivations are more likely to be directed at reducing the problem to a point where it can be tolerated than in effecting fundamental change. In any event we suggest that a relatively small amount of problem reduction, which is likely to occur fairly soon, usually restores the client's equilibrium sufficiently to bring interest in further change below the threshold necessary to sustain his commitment to further remedial action. As clinicians we may regard this degree of change as insufficient, trivial, or epiphenomenal. The affected individual himself may acknowledge that he still has a serious problem. But the point is he may not wish to do anything further about it, after a modest amount of change has relieved his motivational pressure.

If what we have said is true of the majority of clients who seek help at our agencies, we have then a natural model of individual help-seeking and problem reduction that fits much better to short-term than long-term treatment designs. If the period in which change is most likely to occur is the short interval it takes for a rebalancing of the client's problem-coping machinery, then brief treatment should logically be our dominant therapeutic modality.

EMPIRICAL SUPPORT

What evidence do we have for these suppositions? Unfortunately not much that is directly to the point since there has been little study of problem changes *per se*. Moreover, most of the research that can be brought to bear involves changes associated with programs of intervention, making it impossible to sort out characteristics of problem-change in their natural form, so to speak, from change resulting from treatment effects. Nevertheless, available evidence does tend, in our judgment, to support our view.

First, it may be instructive to reexamine some fairly well-known facts about the actual duration of treatment in the light of our hypothesis that problem-change occurs rapidly. If this hypothesis has validity we would expect to find that most individuals who seek interpersonal help will terminate their contacts within a few months. This seems to be the case.

After reviewing studies of continuance in treatment, Garfield (1971) concludes: "It is apparent that, contrary to the usual expectations concerning the length of psychotherapy, most clinic clients are done with it after a few interviews. In practically all of the clinics studied, this pattern . . . was not the result of a deliberately planned brief therapy. *Rather in most instances the patient failed to return for a scheduled appointment"* (p. 275; Garfield's italics).

Among Garfield's sources of evidence for these statements are ten "representative studies" of psychiatric clinics and a survey published by the National Center for Health Statistics (1966). In the representative studies used by Garfield, there were only three out of ten clinics in which the average course of treatment exceeded six interviews. The survey revealed that almost a million Americans consulted a psychiatrist during the twelve-month period from July, 1963 to June, 1964. The average number of visits per person was approximately five. Garfield also notes that "on the basis of limited evidence it appears that those who terminate therapy early rarely go on to seek help elsewhere" (p. 275).

Fowler (1967) comes to similar conclusions concerning the length of treatment in "casework and counseling" agencies: "Despite many sources of noncomparability, the reported rates of nonreturn to a second interview, which range from 15 to 66 percent, tend to cluster around 33 percent. About 33 percent of accepted clientele is lost after two or three interviews and about 33 percent continues into four or more" (p. 271).

These estimates conform closely to data reported by the Family Service Association of America on termination from casework in family service agencies. These data are of particular interest since they pertain exclusively to casework, and are based on statistical reports of several hundred agencies. In 1969, the FSAA reported that in its typical (median) agency, 72 percent of the families receiving one in-person casework interview terminated service prior to the sixth interview.

Such diverse sources of evidence are difficult to aggregate, given varying definitions of "drop out," "treatment," and the like, but some generalizations are possible. Translating interviews into time, it is fair to say that the majority of individuals who seek professional help for social and psychological problems—probably the great majority—remain actively engaged in interpersonal treatment for a period not exceeding three months. Traditionally the results of continuance studies have been viewed with concern, if not dismay. Early termination usually has been interpreted as a premature "dropping out" from treatment, before much has been accomplished, an interpretation based on the assumption that a substantial period of time is needed before interpersonal treatment can be effective. Eiduson (1968) presents the prevailing view when she refers to the "shockingly high incidence of the drop-out problem" as signifying an "acute retreat from help" (p. 919).

A rather different interpretation may be placed on the findings of continuance studies. That most individuals leave treatment early may be seen as a reflection of the natural, rapid processes that serve to blunt the edges of the discomfort that prompts help-seeking. It has been said often that "discontinuers" lack motivation for sustained help. We readily agree with this somewhat tautological assertion, but the reason for the lack of motivation may be found in problem-changes that occur between application and termination. These interpretations are strengthened by the findings of follow-up studies of clients who terminate after only a few interviews. For example, in a study of 166 short-contact cases, which were followed up from three to six months after termination, Kogan (1957) found that the majority of clients reported that their initial problems had at least partially cleared up.

Let us now consider another source of evidence. If the greatest amount of change in psychosocial problems occurs rapidly, one would expect certain results from experiments in which outcomes for subjects receiving treatment limited to a few months are compared with outcomes for comparable subjects receiving treatment of longer duration. Namely, one would expect recipients of the briefer treatment to experience at least as much problem reduction as do their counterparts receiving long-term treatment. Only a few experiments of this type have been reported, but all of them, without any exceptions that we know of, yield results that conform to this expectation.

For example, in a four-year study reported by Reid and Shyne (1969), 120 families who had sought help at a social agency for largely chronic problems in family relations were randomly assigned to two treatment conditions: the one, a planned, short-term casework limited to eight interviews within a three- to four-month period; the other, open-ended, long-term casework. In the short-term program, service was almost uniformly completed within the prescribed limits, while families receiving long-term treatment continued on the average about twice as long. Outcome data obtained at case closing consisted of the client's own assessments, of ratings of researchers who interviewed the clients, of independent judges who listened to the tapes of the research interviewers and, finally, of the judgments of the practitioners themselves, all of whom were trained, experienced caseworkers. Assessments covered not only changes in family problems but also changes in the psychological and social functioning. The results from these varied sources of data were quite consistent. On several key measures of problem and individual change, the clients receiving the briefer service achieved significantly more positive change than clients receiving the longer service. Findings in the other direction were not found. On no measure of change, of almost a hundred employed, did clients receiving long-term treatment have significantly better outcomes. While many conclusions may be drawn from these results, the one central to our present argument is this: the longer time span provided to continued-service clients did not enable them to achieve any more change than was achieved by short-term clients in a much briefer period. The change curve that might be drawn on the basis of the overall findings would show a sharp rise following the beginning of the client's problem-solving efforts followed by a downward slope within a few months.

Results from other experimental or quasi-experimental studies of this type, namely those reported by Phillips and Johnston (1954), Blenkner (1964), Muench (1964), and Schlien (1966), bring one to a similar conclusion. In each of these studies (which are reviewed in greater detail in Reid and Shyne, 1969) clients and patients receiving planned short-term treatment had outcomes as good as, or better than, their counterparts who received treatment of longer duration.

That alleviation in problems of living tends to be a rapid, rather than lengthy process, gains broader support from non-comparative studies of short-term treatment (Murray and Smitson, 1963; Avnet, 1965; Bellak and Small, 1965; Kaffman, 1965; Hare, 1966; Gottschalk, Meyerson, and Gottlieb, 1967; Parad and Parad, 1968b; Shaw, Blumenfeld, and Senf, 1968; Uhlenhuth and Duncan, 1968). These studies, in aggregate, examined outcomes of over 4,000 individuals and families receiving brief, time-limited casework and psychotherapy for the gamut of psychological and interpersonal problems that adults bring to social agencies and mental health facilities. Courses of treatment in the great majority of cases were fewer than fifteen interviews, and as best can be determined, less than four months. Although change measures used were often crude and difficult to compare, the overall proportion of cases reported as "improved" (or the equivalent) was in excess of 70 percent—which compares favorably with improvement rates reported for long-term treatment (Eysenck, 1966; Bergin, 1971). Post-treatment follow-ups conducted in most of these studies, as well as in the comparative studies cited above, indicate that changes associated with brief treatment are relatively durable. In addition, the findings from these studies suggest that only a relatively small proportion of individuals receiving brief therapy turn to more extended forms of help upon its completion.

One of these studies (Uhlenhuth and Duncan, 1968) is of particular interest since it provides data on patient change during the course of brief treatment and more precise measures than are usually obtained about the amount and direction of change. The patients (n = 128) had sought help from an outpatient clinic for emotional problems, such as anxiety and depression, in most cases precipitated by interpersonal difficulties. The patients completed symptom checklists, among other instruments, during intervals between interviews. Seventy-two percent of the patients showed some relief of distress by the end of treatment, which averaged about six weekly interviews. Change in level of distress for the group as a whole assumed the form of a downward curve, with the greatest amount of relief experienced between the first and second weeks. These results, based on six or so replicated measures over time, provide strong evidence that homeostatic mechanisms were operating in a rapid and consistent way to restore emotional equilibrium. By the end of treatment the overall reduction in symptomatic distress was 22 percent. We would argue that such a decline in distress might well be sufficient to restore the individual to a state of balance or at least to eliminate his effective motivation for further help. Although measurements were confined largely to the patients' perceived discomfort, it is precisely this kind of discomfort, in our judgment, that provides the primary motivational push for treatment. Since the therapists were medical students without extensive training or experience in psychotherapy, it does not seem plausible that the changes were the product of exceptional therapeutic skill.

On the basis of the kind of findings we have reviewed, it has been argued that short-term treatment should be the standard treatment modality (Phillips and Weiner, 1966; Parad and Parad, 1968b; Reid, 1970). The argument has been based on the pragmatic grounds that brief treatment appears to be more efficient than long-term treatment since it seems to accomplish comparable results with less expenditure of resources. While large-scale use of brief treatment methods can be amply justified on these practical grounds, the findings we have reviewed also support a theory of change which may explain why brief treatment may be the more efficient modality.

We assume that the several thousand patients and clients treated in these projects are more similar, than dissimilar, to the typical clienteles of casework. While the caseloads in most studies may have been shaped by certain selection criteria, these criteria seemed generally to be used to eliminate a minority of cases that might have been judged as inappropriate for brief treatment rather than to "cream off" a small proportion of cases that might be viewed as particularly suitable for this approach. Moreover, studies that did not use selection criteria tended to be similar in overall results to those that did.

If one now assumes that the changes reported were a function of the therapeutic methods employed, one emerges with a strong case for brief treatment. But that assumption is unrealistic in light of what is generally known of the effectiveness of interpersonal treatment. It is more reasonable to assume that treatment contributed, in some undetermined measure, to natural processes of change. The evidence can then be interpreted to mean that in most cases problem alleviation occurred within the relatively brief span of time suggested by our theory, that alleviation tended to be durable, and appeared sufficient to obviate need for further help-seeking.

We are not sure to what kind and range of problems these formulations apply, but one point must be kept constantly in mind. We are referring to problems as conceived of by the client himself, and not problem definitions imposed by clinicians. Thus these studies suggest that most clients who come to us with distress from intrapyschic or interpersonal sources will, through one means or another, find relief from their problems within a brief period of time.

A final piece of evidence comes from studies of open-ended treatment. If problems tend to change rapidly and in a positive direction, one would expect to find that the bulk of improvement in long-term therapy would occur relatively early. There is evidence that this is so. In their extensive review of psychotherapy research, Meltzoff and Kornreich (1970) conclude that: "psychotherapy, when successful, achieves its major gains relatively early" (p. 357). On the basis of their follow-up study of 131 out-patients, Strupp, Fox, and Lessler

(1969) state that, "therapeutic change, where it occurred, was perceived [by the patients] as having taken place fairly rapidly once treatment was undertaken and appeared to be lasting" (p. 91). Sacks, Bradley, and Beck (1970) investigated client progress after only five interviews in open-ended treatment cases in a family agency. Their evaluation of detailed worker and client ratings led them to conclude that, "there was substantial and consistent evidence that progress in problem coping and/or functioning did occur within five interviews in about half the cases" (p. 84). In only one case in ten was the balance of change in a negative direction.

In sum, while there is a lack of research on problem-change that is free of treatment effects, the findings of studies of individual and family change associated with treatment suggest that in the majority of cases problem alleviation occurs fairly soon after problem onset. This does not mean, of course, that all problems perceived by clients follow this pattern. Our central argument is that in general the greatest amount of problem-change is likely to occur early and this amount is usually sufficient to restore equilibrium and reduce the client's incentive for further change.

These considerations have led us to view the function of casework as stimulating, quickening, and augmenting the kind of processes that naturally characterize problem-change. With but few exceptions, the success of the caseworker's intervention is dependent upon the existence of these processes in much the same way that medical treatment must rely upon the recuperative powers of the body, and education on the student's ability to learn. If the push for change in target problems is short-lived, then the maximum effectiveness of casework intervention is of equally short duration.

Now clients may continue in casework relationships beyond the point of diminishing problem-change and of diminishing treatment effectiveness. There may remain some client motivation to work on larger problems, the caseworker may hold out the promise that much more can be accomplished if they stick with it, and the relationship itself may provide some psychological comforts to both caseworker and client. In some situations focus for change may be sustained for longer periods of time, accounting perhaps for the occasional very successful long-term case that each of us who has practiced casework can remember with pride and satisfaction. It is perhaps our gratification with this kind of case that causes us to overlook the vastly larger number of cases in which continued treatment does not lead to progressive gains, and to overlook the fact that treatment carried beyond the point of diminishing returns contains certain losses: unrewarded worker and client effort, client dissatisfactions and feelings of failure, unmanageable transference problems, and questionable dependency relationships. We also tend to ignore the reality that it is the client's striving for change that provides the caseworker with the opportunity to stimulate new understanding and action. When this striving comes to an end, the caseworker's technical repertoire soon becomes exhausted as he finds himself repeating once again to his client the same interpretations, the same reassurances, the same advice. Perhaps that is why in one study previously referred to, clinical judges found it impossible to distinguish late from early interviews in long-term cases (Reid and Shyne, 1969).

The length of treatment can be kept short, of course, without the imposition of limits which strike many practitioners as arbitrary and restrictive. Why have such limits and, if we need them, how can they be used to best advantage? The main function they serve in our treatment system, and perhaps in short-term treatment systems generally, is to provide a means of regulating the length of treatment relationships lacking natural end-points. Even though short-term treatment may be directed at relatively specific goals, it is often difficult to determine when such goals have been achieved to a satisfactory degree, particularly when target problems concern interpersonal conflict or role performance. There is always the temptation to try to push the client a little further. If we assume that what will be accomplished will generally be accomplished within a certain time period, then limit-setting in advance provides the client with protection against the vagaries of open-ended relationships. In general one expects relationships between professionals and the persons they serve to have fairly well-defined termination criteria. Usually such criteria are derived from service goals, which in other fields, tend to be more circumscribed: after the disease has been cured, the house built, the case won or lost, service naturally comes to an end. When goals are not bounded, some form of prearranged limits is usually set. A good example is higher education: the amount to be learned about a particular subject may be limitless, so one takes courses of fixed duration to achieve in a partial way certain learning goals related to the subject.

Duration limits have other advantages: they force a concentration of effort on achievable goals, lead to better planning in use of time available, and stimulate both practitioner and client to greater effort. Empirical support for the latter advantage has been summed up by Goldstein, Heller and Sechrest (1966) in their wide-ranging effort to develop research-based hypotheses for therapy. According to these authors, setting time limits introduces a "temporal goal gradient" into the treatment relationship, hence research relating to "goal gradient" effects becomes relevant. Such research has demonstrated that an individual's output tends to increase as an anticipated end point nears, a phenomenon also observed, we might say, among writers working against firm deadlines. As these authors conclude, "the effect of anticipation of termination should be to call forth increased patient and therapist effort toward the therapeutic goal, that is, patient change" (p. 281).

A final point needs to be made: the use of time limits as a standard method of controlling the duration of service does not prevent the offering of long-term service to clients who have completed a course of short-term treatment and who are motivated to go on. If time limits are established at the onset and if treatment is carried out under the continuing expectation that the time limits, with perhaps some adjustments, will be adhered to, available evidence suggests that few clients will in fact opt for long-term treatment. Such an arrangement would enable us to locate those few clients willing and able to use extended help without attempting to drag entire case loads beyond the optimum duration of service.

CHAPTER FIVE

THE CLIENT'S TASK

AN INDIVIDUAL faced with problems of living may react in a variety of ways: he may simply do nothing and wait for time to perform its reputed healing function. He may aggravate his difficulty, as does a person who responds to interpersonal conflict by escalating it. The problem may prove so overwhelming that it creates a general breakdown in functioning. But most individuals sooner or later take constructive action to alleviate their troubles. Tired of the fight, a husband and wife grope for a compromise; a shy man forces himself to take initiatives with women; a depressed person talks things out with a friend; a neglectful father tries to spend more time with his children. Such coping efforts may be seen as natural tasks individuals set for themselves in order to resolve problems. They are not easy to carry out and their execution is seldom completely successful, but they are necessary to survival in the turbulent social world of the average person. Our treatment system is built upon this kind of constructive responsiveness to problems. Our model is largely an attempt to enhance the natural task-setting and task-achieving of individuals in difficulty.

The use of the term "task" to describe human responses to troublesome life situations is not new. In an effort to describe its usage in social work Bartlett (1970) observes that, "the task concept is a way of describing the demands made upon people by various life situations. These have to do with daily living, such as growing up in the family, learning in school, entering the world of work, marrying and rearing a family and also with the common traumatic situations of life such as bereavement, separation, illness, or financial difficulties" (p. 96). Rhona Rapoport (1963), Lydia Rapoport (1970), and other crisis theorists have employed the term in a similar way to describe action requirements called for by crisis situations. Our use of "task" as a behavioral concept is somewhat broader. It is not confined to points of transition or crisis but is rather applied to the individual's efforts to resolve any problem of living.

"TASK" AS A TREATMENT CONSTRUCT

In the context of interpersonal treatment, the term "task" sometimes refers to the practitioner's actions, sometimes to the client's, and sometimes to both. Schwartz and Sample (1966) viewed the caseworker's service activities as consisting of a set of tasks. Studt (1968) conceives of the task as the "common goal for the worker and the client" and "different kinds of sub-tasks for each." Studt concludes that "one has no choice but to assign priority to the client's goals in defining the tasks and sub-tasks, and to recognize that the onus is on the worker to identify and establish in action the common base of purpose that allows him to achieve his professional goals through the client's pursuit of his" (p. 24).

Studt's conception of "task" is close to ours. Perhaps the main distinction is that we reserve the term for the client's goals and actions. In our usage, a "task" is what the client agrees to attempt to do to alleviate a problem. Usually the client's task can be expressed in a single sentence: Mrs. Allen is to develop a more accurate understanding of her child's behavior; Mr. Cardo is to secure a job that would enable him to support himself and his family; Henry is to work out arrangements with his school so that he can keep up with his studies while he is in the hopsital. More than one task may be worked on simultaneously or in sequence, or reciprocal or shared tasks may be used in work with couples and families.

This construct is well suited to our treatment system for a number of reasons. Most important it provides a theoretical link between the client's problem and the caseworker's intervention. By definition, a target problem is one that the client can act on directly on his own or indirectly through the caseworker. Furthermore, according to our formulations, the client's actions provide the central means of problem-change. Hence it becomes essential to define with the client what course of action might be most effective in resolving his problem. The caseworker's treatment strategy then is directed to helping the client carry out this course of action, which is called "the task."

In turn, the view that the caseworker's central function is to help the client achieve his task, accomplishes additional purposes. It helps the caseworker focus his intervention on a specific goal, an essential requirement in planned, short-term treatment. It also gives the client a sense of self-direction in problem-solving. While the task may have been formulated with the help of the caseworker, it represents action that makes sense to the client, and it is his to carry out. He may make considerable use of the caseworker's help, but he uses this help as a means of accomplishing his own objective. Finally, the client can get a clear grasp of the purposes and strategies of treatment and of his own role in it, a special advantage for clients who do not readily grasp the means and ends of casework. The task, which he and the caseworker formulate, defines what he is to do and the caseworker's intervention can be expressly related to helping him do it.

The general usefulness of task as a treatment construct has been illustrated in Studt's (1968) work with adult offenders. Her comments have general applicability:

Assigning priority to the question of what is the client's task gave us a touchstone to distinguish between professional help to a *client* and the benign super-imposition of an expert's values and perspectives on a captive *recipient of service*. It restored the client, in both theory and practice, to the dignity of his rightful position as primary worker in task accomplishment. It recognized explicitly, in the basic conceptual framework, the brute fact that no one but the client can perform the tasks required by his own life stage and particular situation. Further, it properly emphasized the secondary and indirect nature of 'helping,' correcting for the natural human tendency of any expert to perceive his own orientations as better informed and more wisely conceived than those of his client. And finally this position proved to have a salutary effect on our own self image as professional helpers, because it substituted the humility of a probabilistic set of expectations about what can be accomplished by any professional intervention into natural life sequences, for the somewhat over-weening and less flexible assumption that there is a direct causal relationship between specific professional actions and change in the client's life. (p. 42)

We assume, as do most advocates of short-term approaches, that progress clients achieve in brief, time-limited treatment can serve as a stimulus for further constructive changes after treatment has ended. The concentration of treatment effort on the client's task achievement might be expected to strengthen such after-effects. If the client achieves the agreed-upon task or makes substantial progress toward it, then he has been able to demonstrate to himself that he is able to effect change and perhaps how change can best be effected.

We are often asked, "How does the idea of 'task' relate to the usual notion of treatment goals?" In our formulation, "task" refers both to means and ends. Any event can be viewed through this double lens. If we see the event as a future state toward which we are striving, then it becomes a goal. It can also be seen, however, as the means of accomplishing still another future state. We are referring here to the notion of a "means-ends chain" (Simon, 1957). Whether an event is labeled as a goal or an instrumentality depends entirely on how the event is construed.

Let us suppose the client's task is to leave her mother's household. Her leaving may then become the immediate and controlling *goal* of treatment. At the same time the accomplishment of that task becomes the *means* to alleviate the problem which, let us say, is one of interpersonal conflict between the client and the mother. Now one might have said the goal of treatment was to help the client move away from her mother, but to put it so would ignore the fact that the moving away was also a means to achieving another goal, reducing interpersonal conflict; to say that her effecting a separation was only a means to alleviate the problem ignores the fact that this is something to be achieved, hence a goal. The task construct provides a way of specifying and designating pivotal client actions, whose achievement can be viewed as the major goal of treatment but which also serve the major means of accomplishing the superordinate goal of problem alleviation.

TASK AND TARGET PROBLEM

The course of action that a client may take to resolve his problem is suggested by the definition of the problem itself. If the client's problem is specified as inadequate performance at work, then his task would normally have to do with improving his performance. The problem and task can, of course, be defined at the same level of generality. Thus, a couple's problem may be defined as conflict over financial matters, and they might assume as their task the resolution of the conflict. If this were done the difference between problem and task would be largely a matter of wording. Task formulation then would represent little advance over problem specification. We require, therefore, that the task be defined at a more specific level than the problem. Thus, if the problem were defined as a couple's conflict over financial matters, their task might be to work out a budget together.

While the specific problems and tasks will vary from case to case, some generalizations can be made about the kind of task associated with a given problem category. These generalizations need much further development but they present some guidelines that may be of use and indicate some directions for further work on the model.

Tasks directed at a problem of interpersonal conflict are perhaps the most complex since, by definition, two individuals share the problem. As a general rule the task, or tasks, must also involve two individuals. As suggested earlier (chapter 3) if one partner in an *apparent* problem of interpersonal conflict is not willing to participate in treatment, then the *target* problem is better defined as a problem in the role performance of the client who will be seen.

Tasks involving partners in conflict call for each to behave in ways more acceptable to the other. To the extent they are able to do so, conflict should be reduced. Such tasks may either be *shared* or *reciprocal*. A shared task calls for both partners to work closely together toward achieving the same immediate objective: for example, they may be asked to work out an agreement about how the children are to be disciplined or to decide on how the family's income is to be spent. Reciprocal tasks are two interrelated tasks divided between the two partners. A husband may try to keep from contradicting his wife's directions to the children, but his wife will attempt to be more consistent in her handling (one of the reasons for the husband's interference). Or a father's task may be to spend more time with his son while the son works on behaving in a less provocative way toward his father. Tasks may be structured to be worked on either inside or outside the interview, or both. Or they may be devised to be carried out under natural conditions, such as in the client's home, with the practitioner present. For example, the task for a couple might be to resolve a particular issue through discussing it without introducing provocative and irrelevant messages such as references to one another's "personality problems." While the couple may work on such a task outside the interview, the caseworker's active participation may be necessary if they are to make any progress. Thus the task might be worked on primarily within the interview. A task involving conflict between parents over a child's behavior might be worked on in a series of sessions in the home involving *in vivo* interactions between the parents over the child's behavior.

Families may suffer from interlocking problems of conflict involving more than two members. The parent's dissension over the behavior of their adolescent daughter may be interlocked with a conflict between the mother and daughter. A set of reciprocal tasks for each of the family members might be devised for this set of problems.

Problems in dissatisfaction with social relations generally lead to tasks which require the client to modify certain patterns in his social behavior. Often novel forms of behavior, with attendant risk-taking, are demanded. The task spells out the behaviors to be undertaken. Thus Mr. Drew (who has a problem of loneliness) will take initiatives, such as joining a social club, to make friends. It is assumed that much of the treatment work will be concerned with obstacles, often internal, preventing the client from taking actions to relieve his dissatisfactions. While such tasks have their inner aspects, their focus is on change in the client's overt behavior. One would not develop tasks addressed primarily to discovery of the reasons for the client's lack of gratification in his social relations.

Problems that clients may have with formal organizations assume a wide variety of forms and hence many task possibilities arise. Often tasks involve a client's taking some action to bring about a change in the provision of some service or resource. (Presumably the client has made some attempt to bring about such a change but has encountered difficulties;

otherwise the *problem* to be addressed would not be classified as his *relations* with a formal organization but rather as inadequate resources.) In tasks of this kind, further action on the client's part may need to be carried forward by the caseworker acting as the client's agent or advocate. Although the client makes use of the caseworker's skills as a mediator and his knowledge of formal organizations, the task remains the client's. A quite different kind of task emerges from strains between organizations and "captive" clients, such as patients in hospitals, inmates in institutions, or offenders on probation or parole. The client's behavior may be deviating from the rules or norms of the organization or the organization may be expecting him to behave in a way he does not wish to. Generally the client's task in such situations is to take action that will help him improve his position vis-à-vis the organization. To do so he may need to alter his own behavior, but the organization may need to give as well and the client, with the caseworker's help, may try to alter the organization's point of view on the behavior of its members. In order to avoid an unwanted transfer a soldier may need to "shape-up" but at the same time his company commander may need to revise his perception of the soldier as a "born goof-up." A juvenile offender's only perceived problem may be the restrictions on his mobility because he is on probation. His task in brief treatment might be to find a better way of coping with the restrictions, a task that might include trying to get them modified.

In any case, the caseworker takes his initiative from the client and attempts to serve the client's interests in relation to the organization. The caseworker's responsibility is not to help the client conform to organizational requirements, although greater conformity may be the result of the client's attempt to resolve his problem. Even if the caseworker is employed by the organization with which the problem is occurring, he is better viewed as the client's representative than as a protector of the organization's interest.

Difficulties in role performance are likely to give rise to tasks concerned with gaps between the client's expectations and performance in carrying out role behaviors. While the tasks are stated in behavioral terms, for example, a father is to spend more time with his son, attention must be given to the client's self-expectations since they obviously define the boundaries of the task. If a mother is to be less dominating with her son, then it is important to clarify what she thinks her behavior with her son should be like, and to consider with her the need for change in these expectations if such change seems necessary for progress on the task to occur.

Consideration of tasks involving role performance provide us with a good opportunity to make two general points which have been made in other contexts but bear repeating. First, the ideas we have sketched out concerning role performance tasks are rudimentary in the extreme. They illustrate one of the many knowledge limitations of the present model and one of the kinds of limitations encountered in any general model at an early stage of development. We have not yet reached the point where we can lay out in any thorough way the various task possibilities (and related considerations) for any given problem. Second, a good deal has been written which is germane to the formulation and execution of tasks involving role performance. The writings of Perlman, particularly *Persona* (1968), are especially applicable. Our hope at this juncture is that we have provided users of the model with a structure that will permit them to make use of the existing literature in helping clients develop tasks in relation to all problem categories.

Since problems of social transition have at their core some actual impending, or potential, shift in the client's social situation, related tasks are concerned with whether or not certain changes are to be made or how certain changes are to be managed. If the client is faced with a choice about a potential change, then his task may be to make the appropriate choice. Thus the task for the girl who is unmarried and pregnant might be to decide whether to keep or surrender her child. The task for a woman who has learned that her husband intends to leave her might be to decide whether to fight to keep him or to find a satisfactory way to live without him.

When the client has already decided on a given change, or has no choice about it, then his task may be largely concerned with planning how the change can best be effected, as in the case of a patient or inmate about to be discharged. In other situations the client's task or tasks may be directed at coping with changes that have taken place or are in the process of occurring. Thus, the family that has just migrated to a new locale may need to work on tasks that assist its members to effect a satisfactory transition.

We have indicated that the problem classification scheme used in this model is imperfect and overlapping. How one classifies the problem tends to direct the area in which one seeks the task. Doubtful and uncertain instances abound, necessitating that both client and caseworker make a judgment as to what element in the problem pattern appears most important to the client at the time, understanding that there is nothing immutable about either the classification of a problem or the formulation of a task. However, additional issues are encountered in respect to problems of emotional distress.

Most clients experiencing problems of daily living are distressed. It is sometimes difficult to determine whether the client most wants help with the distress *per se* or with the problem that has precipitated it. If the former is clearly decided upon, then the client's task, broadly speaking, becomes to alleviate or resolve his disturbing feelings. For certain kinds of distress the passage of time or events may be the major determinants of change, although the client may gain relief from unburdening his feelings. If the client is depressed over the loss of a loved one or anxious over impending surgery, his specific task may be to talk over his thoughts and feelings with the caseworker. Usually, however, attention is directed to what the client can do beyond this to alleviate his distress. In some cases the task might be directed to increasing his understanding of the precipitating event and of his own reactions to it. In other cases, some overt action on the client's part, either addressed to the precipitator, (if it is still active) or carried out as a means of helping him express or rechannel his feelings might constitute the basis of the task.

Problems of inadequate resources lead straightforwardly in most cases to tasks concerned with obtaining the resources needed. As in tasks addressed to problems of relations with formal organizations, the caseworker may serve as the client's agent in locating and securing the needed resources, as the client defines the need. If the caseworker or his agency controls the needed resources, the client's task can be carried out through cooperating in whatever eligibility procedures may be required. As we suggest in chapter 10 client tasks of this kind might be more appropriately carried out with the assistance of clerical and administrative personnel, than with the help of caseworkers. Caseworkers can perhaps make better use of their skills in respect to tasks characterized by greater uncertainty: for example if the desired resources are not easily obtained, if their existence is questionable, or if it is not clear what kind of resources the client wants or in what amount.

GUIDELINES FOR SHAPING THE TASK

Normally the task evolves from the client's own problem-solving efforts and intentions. The caseworker's function is to help the client shape the best possible course of action to remedy his difficulty. In carrying out this function, the practitioner is guided by certain criteria which will now be considered.

THE CLIENT'S MOTIVATION. What the client wants to do about his problem and how much he wants to do it represent dual aspects of the client's motivation (Ripple, 1963) that must be considered in task-centered work. Shaping of the task generally follows the direction and force of the client's motivation. The practitioner attempts to determine what the client thinks he should do about the problem and tries to formulate task possibilities consonant with the client's own push for change. It is assumed that the client's motivation is the most potent factor in problem reduction and, hence, must be utilized to the fullest. The strongest empirical support for this assumption is provided by Ripple (1963) who found that motivational factors were better predictors of case outcome than other classes of factors studied.

The client cannot be expected to write his own ticket, however. In some cases he may not be able to think of a promising course of action or may be floundering among a number of possibilities. In other cases his ideas may be unrealistic or their implementation might require resources that the caseworker cannot provide. In general the practitioner's expert knowledge of the kind of task that may be particularly useful for a given problem may help the client develop a course of action more effective than any he might have thought of on his own. The caseworker's inputs may be particularly needed in problems of interpersonal conflict in which possible discrepant motivations between the partners need to be reconciled and in which the clients, because of their subjective involvements, are not able to perceive what actions on their part may be most fruitful.

We are willing, however, to meet the client more than halfway—to assume, unless there is strong evidence to the contrary, that his plan of action offers a valid basis for his task, even though we may have misgivings about it. If we steer him in other directions we should have good reasons for so doing and should so inform him.

The essential requirement is to arrive at a task to which the client is willing to commit his effort. If the task has been suggested by the worker then we assume it is one that makes sense to the client and one he is willing to pursue, even though he may have reservations about it.

Certain clients may appear to be motivated for more than they can be expected to accomplish in a course of task-centered casework. A husband and wife may ask for help with conflicts cutting across all aspects of their relationship, or a shy, inhibited person may want to be the life of the party. Many such clients turn out, of course, to be willing to concentrate their efforts on some specific goal they wish to pursue, yet some will hold to more global objectives. It is true that the process of problem specification, with an accompanying explanation of the nature and limits of treatment, should serve to ready clients for work on specific aspects of their difficulty, but the client with far-reaching goals may still be reluctant to confine his efforts to a specific task, particularly when he realizes that work on this task will be pretty much the sum and substance of this particular treatment experience.

How do we square task-centered treatment for such a client with the value we accord the client's request? If we have no right to give clients more help than they ask for, is it proper to give them less than we are able to? We can repeat, of course, what we have said and documented elsewhere, that in most cases concentrated time-limited work on a specific problem will accomplish as much if not more than will an extended approach addressed to a range of problems. This position and the reasons for it can be made clear to the client. If he remains unconvinced, two choices can be offered: that he try the task-centered approach with the option of receiving additional help if he finds short-term treatment to be insufficient or that he turn immediately to a form of treatment more compatible with his own request. The evidence we have presented (chapter 4) suggests that few clients would take the second choice. A frank discussion of the alternatives should help the client with questions about brief treatment to make a more rational decision.

FEASIBILITY OF THE TASK. A task may be well related to the target problem and the client's motivation to work on it may be high, but it may not prove feasible to carry out. It may demand certain kinds of behavioral changes that the client is not capable of making, obstacles in his social field may prove too formidable, or the caseworker and his agency may lack the necessary resources to help him.

"Impossible" tasks can be modified or discarded of course, but there is little point in starting to work on something that offers little chance of success. The caseworker does have a responsibility to use his knowledge to help the client select a feasible task and to inform the client if he thinks a task is not workable.

In making his assessment of the feasibility of tasks the caseworker uses data he has collected from the client and others in the course of problem exploration and identification. He will have made numerous observations of the client's behavior and will have formed certain judgments about his intellectual abilities, his ability to plan and follow through, his way of handling emotions, and his manner of relating to others. Characteristics associated with his socioeconomic position and ethnic identification will have been noted, as well as restrictions of his capacities resulting from serious physical illness or marked maladaptive tendencies. In cases involving problems of family relations, particularly in which family members have been seen together, the caseworker will have formed some impressions of family interaction.

Such information will be selective and incomplete, since it will have been obtained in the course of discussing the client's problem rather than systematically elicited through a prearranged schedule of questions. Nevertheless it should provide the practitioner with some basis for a judgment about task feasibility. Moreover, since he is usually concentrating on a limited range of task possibilities, he can elicit necessary supplementary data with a minimum of inquiry.

Presumably these observations will be related to the practitioner's general knowledge, resulting in certain diagnostic hypotheses about the feasibility of a given task. While in this model the practitioner is free to use whatever kinds of knowledge he sees fit to make sense out of his observations, our predilection is toward use of "low order" concepts closely based on observed behavior. We suggest cautious use of global concepts such as ego strength, reality testing, character disorder, and the like, which require fairly elaborate inferences to be made about a person's behavior. As Stuart (1970) has suggested, there is a good deal of evidence that such "dispositional" concepts have poor reliability (that is, experts are likely to disagree when applying them) even when a good deal of information is available. In our model, and in short-term approaches generally, the practitioner's data about the client are quite limited. Usually not enough is known about the client's behavior in general to warrant use of terms describing his ego, personality or psychopathology. Even when concepts at this level are helpful in explaining client behavior, they may be of little value in making predictions about it. As Dubin (1969) has observed, concepts may have useful explanatory functions but may lack predictive power. Assessments of task feasibility, of course, are based in large part on predictions of the client's actions. Thus the concept of "paranoid tendencies" may help explain a client's excessive suspiciousness but may not help us predict whether or not the client will succeed on a job.

In our judgment the practitioner's assessment of what the client is able to accomplish should be tied as closely as possible to what he has observed or to reasonably valid data he has collected. Inferences should be kept to a minimum. The caseworker might well decide that a client who has received failing grades in high-school English and demonstrated a lack of facility with words in the interview stands a poor chance of succeeding in a court stenographer's training program and may convey his reservations to her. We would hope the caseworker would not discourage a client from her wish to leave her mother because of his impression that the client's "dependency needs" were too strong to enable her to do so.

In most cases the practitioner's questions about feasibility serve to help the client shape or modify the task rather than to discourage him from pursuing it at all. In this process we recommend that the practitioner view the client's potentials in an optimistic light, with emphasis upon his capacities for constructive action rather than upon his limitations or pathology. The expressions "why not" and "let's try" better convey the spirit of the model than "one cannot expect too much because. . . ."

DESIRABILITY OF THE TASK. Consideration of the feasibility of a task comes down to the question, "Can it be done?" When we consider its desirability, the question becomes, "Should it be done?" The latter question is likely to arise when the caseworker thinks that carrying out a given task will have certain negative consequences for the client, himself or others. If a client is helped to achieve his goal of immediate discharge from a mental hospital, will he be "better or worse off"? An alcoholic mother wants her children, currently in placement, returned to her. Will this be good for the children? How the practitioner answers such questions, and what he does with his answers, depends not only on his knowledge of consequences of certain actions but also the value he places on the client's right to make his own decisions, even when those decisions may have consequences that the practitioner, his agency and others deem undesirable.

If we hold that the caseworker's efforts should be directed at meeting the expressed, considered request of the client, then our own solutions for such dilemmas take a particular course. First of all, we give the caseworker the opportunity as well as the obligation to challenge tasks the client might propose which the caseworker would regard as undesirable in their consequences. But this should be done in a forthright manner, with the caseworker making explicit the consequences he foresees and why he thinks they are undesirable. Here one is reminded that among social workers the term "casework" is sometimes used as a verb connoting a devious attempt on the part of one professional to discourage another, usually a subordinate, from doing something through use of pseudo-therapeutic and indirect methods of influence. If caseworkers resent being "caseworked," perhaps clients do also. The client deserves to know clearly where the caseworker stands; at least then the client has the opportunity to discuss his proposed course of action *on its merits*.

Let us suppose that the client, after his discussion with the caseworker, persists in his request—now a considered request —that they pursue a task the caseworker still thinks might have undesirable consequences. Our hope is that the caseworker, keeping in mind that his predictions are highly uncertain at best and taking an optimistic view of the client's capacities, would not let his reservations stand in the way of his helping the client with the task. There may be risks but these can be faced with the client.

A caseworker cannot be expected, however, to commit himself to helping the client achieve a goal whose value he seriously questions. If this is the case, he should inform the client who may then wish to seek other sources of assistance. There are other exceptions and, of course, many gray areas. The caseworker cannot lend his support to proposed tasks that would lead him or the client into illegal activities. Certain types of clients, such as children, the severely mentally retarded, and the overtly psychotic may lack the mental faculties to make responsible decisions or to appraise their consequences. And, of course, one can easily find dilemmas to which no general principles seem to apply, for example in cases in which one family member's goal may have undesirable consequences for another, and both are the caseworker's clients.

SUB-TASKS AND MULTIPLE TASKS. As we have indicated, more than one task may be developed in a particular case. Let us now take up some general considerations involved in selection and organization of a plurality of tasks.

At the simplest level of task organization are cases in which there is only one target problem and only one task. From any single task, however, one can derive *sub-tasks,* or client actions whose accomplishment is necessary to achieve the overall task. For example, a client whose task is to locate and gain admission to a suitable home for the aging may need to carry out a number of discrete activities, or sub-tasks, related to the overall task. One might consist of making a decision about a home to enter on the basis of information supplied by the caseworker; another might involve making arrangements to dispose of personal property prior to admission. At this point we see the notion of sub-tasks as useful in helping the practitioner and client organize their efforts in the implementation of complex tasks. It also may be of value in "mapping out" the kinds of discrete client activities that are to be expected in certain kinds of general tasks, such as entering and leaving institutions.

Since each target problem generally requires its own task, multiple tasks occur when more than one problem is dealt with. Also, more than one general task can be developed for a single problem. We can identify two patterns of multiple tasks: *concurrent* and *sequential*. Concurrent tasks are worked on simultaneously as in the case of the client with dispersed problems who may divide his efforts among two or more tasks. Sequential tasks are those carried out one after the other. In some cases a sequence of tasks may be planned at the outset, in relation to one or more problems. In others, a sequence may evolve as the initial task is carried out as far as is practical and is replaced by another.

In any short-term treatment design one must constantly struggle with the question of what can be accomplished within a relatively brief and fixed period. This question is basic to all others in thinking about patterns of multiple tasks. On the one hand, the practitioner and client may confine themselves to a single task when additional tasks could be profitably undertaken. On the other hand, both may find themselves swamped by an excessive load of tasks, with the result that little is accomplished on any one. The latter danger seems to be the more common, particularly with clients who present a number of problems.

Unfortunately we have no well-established principles at this point that would help determine how many tasks of what kind constitute a maximum load for the model. Our experience thus far suggests that it is usually best to concentrate on a single task (or two closely related tasks) if significant behavioral changes on the part of the client are required. Tasks addressed to alleviation of problems of interpersonal conflict, dissatisfactions in social relations, and role performance fall into this category. While tasks addressed to remaining problems are more likely to lend themselves to multiple patterns, even here perhaps two or three concurrent tasks seem to constitute a maximum load in the great majority of cases. Our experience with task sequences have been too limited to provide a basis for comment.

The requests of most clients, we think, can be met (to the extent it is possible to satisfy such requests through casework) within the structure of tasks set forth above. Problems of excessive task loads are most likely to arise, in our judgment, when the caseworker leads the client to undertake more tasks than either can manage. In short-term work the practitioner must be satisfied to help his client significantly in a limited area of his life and must credit the client's capacity to manage problems in other areas.

OPEN TASKS AND CLOSED TASKS. In the clinical trials of the model, it was found helpful to classify tasks as "open" or "closed." An open task has no natural point of termination. "To make new friends" is an example of an open task, since one could go on making new friends indefinitely. By contrast, a closed task has a fixed end point; it can be unequivocally completed. "To join a social club" or to "enroll in school" are examples of closed tasks. The distinction seems to be of some use in setting durational limits. Paradoxically, limits can be more firmly set for open tasks since they are by definition interminable; an arbitrary end point set in advance makes sense. Working toward a firm termination date, if it is possible to do so, probably does heighten the goal gradient effect referred to earlier. Greater flexibility may be called for in respect to closed tasks since the practitioner may wish to adjust the limits of treatment to the natural end point, if possible. Thus, if the client's task were to find a job, one might relate the projected length of treatment to some estimate of how long it might take the client to find work, with allowances made for some shifting of the terminal interview or date depending on the client's progress. One might not wish to end treatment with successful completion of the task just around the corner. On the other hand, there is no reason to dispense with time limits for closed tasks. Since most tasks of this type normally can be completed within the span of time called for in the model, time limits can be used to establish an outer limit that may help prevent procrastination and excessive delay on the part of both client and caseworker.

TASK FORMULATION. Formulation of the task may be reached through many routes. The caseworker may simply affirm a task the client himself presents or may suggest a task which the client accepts. Most often a statement of the task will emerge from a process of give-and-take between the caseworker and client as they consider what can be done about the problem. Whatever path is used the caseworker should state clearly what he believes the client's task to be and should make sure that he and the client agree on the formulation. Normally the task can be summarized in one or two sentences:

"Your job then will be to iron out your differences about how to deal with your son's troublesome behavior." (To a couple.)

"You want to be able to make appropriate demands of other people: this is what we will work on."

"I will try to help you get someone to take care of you and the children following your surgery."

In each of these examples, the client's task is stated. The caseworker then seeks confirmation of the statement and takes up possible misunderstandings between himself and the client. Each statement, of course, requires clarification and specification, a process that normally is begun as soon as agreement on the general nature of the task is reached.

The last example merits special comment since, from the statement at least, one is not sure what action is expected of the client. In some situations (and this is an example of one) the caseworker may do most of the "doing" because the problem requires considerable caseworker activity. The task is still formulated as the client's, however, with the recognition that the client may use the services of the caseworker as his major means of achieving the task.

If the caseworker has assumed, as we have suggested, an optimistic point of view about the client's capacities, and if the task selected is one the client is motivated to carry out and one whose accomplishment is feasible, then the caseworker's communications to the client about the task should naturally convey his expectations that the client's efforts should be successful.

TASK SELECTION AND FORMULATION: ILLUSTRATIVE CASES. Mr. Todd, twenty-two years old, applied to a psychiatric clinic for help in trying to find out why he persistently failed in school and work. Since he was in a closely supervised, competitive management training program he was particularly concerned over doing well. At the same time, he was not sure that he ought to be so concerned about success since he had other interests which he valued highly, namely interpersonal relations with men and women of his own age and aspirations to participate in group activities to improve social conditions. Mr. Todd was observed to be of above average intelligence, possessed of a good deal of self-awareness, and moderately planful. He suffered from an uncertain self-estimate and guilt about his past failures in college and in a previous job. He was easily distracted from his work, ignoring his duties in favor of extensive social contacts on the job which led him into complex and troublesome relationships outside working hours. Despite the gratifications he derived from them, his social relationships were fraught with a variety of problems, including resentment of his girl friend's dependency on him and his own tendency to be overdependent on older men.

Because Mr. Todd said that his deepest concern was over his work problems, his problem was classified as one of role performance and specified as work underachievement. This classification and specification guided the caseworker to concentrate his communications concerning task selection into the area of what might be done to increase Mr. Todd's achievement at work. Problems in his social relationships would be considered only when they had a demonstrable connection to his work difficulties. With this guidance, Mr. Todd chose to assume responsibility for using the task-centered sequence to achieve an upgrading of his work. His task was to improve his work performance by reducing his distractions. The situation possessed a natural time boundary, for another efficiency report was due on him in fourteen weeks. Hence he was offerred the maximum duration of twelve sessions at weekly intervals. This task fits the general conditions of a single task.

An example of concurrent tasks is provided by the case of Miss L, nineteen, who had been hospitalized for a severe liver illness which would leave her with substantial limitations on her activities. She was referred to the social service department of the hospital because she was unduly agitated and depressed. The problem exploration revealed that although depressed by the circumstances of her illness, Miss L was equally concerned over the prospects of having to return home from the hospital to a disorganized family with a weak, nagging mother whom she resented. She wondered if some arrangement might be made for her to go to a nursing home or a boarding home to live more independently. She was anxious lest her boy friend leave her because of her illness and was worried over what kind of employment she could obtain in view of her physical condition.

All these concerns had a common thread—Miss L's need to be independent yet have satisfactory relations with the two most important people in her life, her mother and her boy friend. She was an intelligent, capable young woman, handicapped by ill health and lack of work skills, coming from an impoverished and disturbed home. Since she was about to be discharged from the hospital and needed to make decisions about her living arrangements, work, and her relationship with her boy friend, her problem was classified as one of social transition. It was decided that her tasks would be to decide whether to go home or elsewhere upon her discharge from the hospital, to scrutinize what her real feelings were about her boy friend, and to plan what she could do in seeking work when her health permitted.

In the case of Mrs. J, a sequence of tasks was developed. A middle-aged, well-educated black woman, she had been caring for her two-year-old grandson for the past year. The child's parents, living in another city, had entrusted the boy to her because they were overwhelmed by his behavior. The family thought the child might be severely retarded. A capable woman, Mrs. J was eager to get help but unable to express her anger at her husband and the parents for failing to clarify how much authority she had for the grandchild. The first task was to secure a diagnosis and recommendations from a child development clinic. It soon became obvious that Mrs. J needed to be relieved of her anger toward the family and acquire authority to act on the child's behalf. The second task became for all the adults to communicate openly what their intentions were about where the child would live and who was responsible. The child's parents came to the city for family interviews, which led to their giving Mrs. J authority to proceed. It was uncertain whether the clinic could provide the child with a program of training and physiotherapy. The final task was to negotiate with the clinic for continuance or referral.

CHAPTER SIX

SYSTEMATIC AND RESPONSIVE
COMMUNICATION

IN TASK-CENTERED casework, interactions between practitioner and client or others are ultimately defined within a communications frame of reference. In our terms "communication" refers to all behaviors that convey meaning. Most are in the form of vocal expressions, but some occur as gestures, facial expressions, and other bodily movements. Our interest lies in the meanings and effects of communication or in what has been called its semantic and pragmatic aspects (Watzlawick, 1967).

Communicative acts constitute the empirical referents of all statements made about caseworker activities within, and outside, the interview. Thus, if we assert that one of the caseworker's treatment methods is to help the client increase his awareness of obstacles to task accomplishment, it is with the understanding that we can produce the specific kinds of practitioner communications that make up this method. Or suppose one were to say (we would probably not say it ourselves) that the "practitioner is relating to a particular client in a maternal manner," before attaching importance to the statement, we would require a specification of those communications presumably signifying maternal qualities. Observations that cannot be pinned down in this way reveal more about the imagery of the observer than the events they purport to describe.

A major reason for using this framework has just been suggested: it provides us with observable, measurable units that can be used to describe what transpires in caseworker-client interaction. It also forces a useful distinction between what the practitioner does on the one hand and, on the other, his intentions, attitudes, feelings, and the like. This distinction was neatly, although unwittingly, illustrated by a student of one of the authors. Her classmates had just rated the degree of empathy she communicated in an interchange with a client and could find little trace of this precious quality. After reluctantly agreeing with the assessment of her peers, she exclaimed, "But I *felt* empathic!" In our view the practitioner's internal state becomes important only as it is communicated to the client and even then its importance is secondary to what is, in fact, communicated. If what a worker communicates is described by the client receiving it and by an independent observer as "warm," then we would say that "warmth" has been communicated, regardless of what the caseworker might have been feeling at the time. The caseworker's inner state obviously affects what he communicates and is important for this reason, but knowledge of it is not central to an analysis of his communication.

Finally, the communications framework provides us with a comprehensive system of concepts and terms by which to describe joint activities of worker and client. More attention is given to the practitioner's than the client's communication since we are presenting guidelines for the practitioner. Such a disproportionate emphasis is not necessarily inconsistent with a communications framework. One can choose to examine a particular element of a communications system more intensively than others, as long as one does not lose sight of how the element selected interacts with others.

Two aspects of practitioner communication are of particular concern in task-centered casework: the immediate apparent goals to which his communicative acts are addressed and certain general qualities of these acts. Classifications of the practitioner's communications according to their immediate, apparent goals lead to the familiar typology of acts that are normally referred to as "treatment techniques"—in our model, exploration, structuring, enhancing awareness, encouragement, and direction. (The caseworker's techniques will be dealt with in detail in the following chapter.) We shall turn first to consider certain qualities of practitioner communication that characterize or cut across these techniques.

Innumerable qualities have been identified as desirable characteristics of practitioner communication. Practitioners are advised to convey warmth, goodwill, tolerance, empathy, acceptance, and so on. Clinical experience, common sense, and some research evidence suggest that such qualities are indeed desirable characteristics of the practitioner's communication. Unfortunately, however, they are seldom put into operational form, so their meanings remain vague, and rarely is the practitioner given a clear idea of how to translate them into practice.

Finally, most of these qualities are expected to be exhibited by practitioners of interpersonal treatment, simply because of the nature of the work. Similarly, we expect that mathematicians will have a liking for numbers and that lawyers will show respect for the law. In constructing a treatment model, there is little advantage in stressing the use of qualities of communication that tend to be generally expected, particularly if they do not lend themselves to discriminating measurement. It makes more sense to emphasize those qualities that may be distinctive of the model under construction or that may assume special forms within that model. In that way the model builder can concentrate his energies measuring specific qualities whose value may then be tested through empirical methods.

Let us now turn our attention to two communication qualities we regard as particularly important in our model. As we shall see, both are specifications of certain aspects of the general qualities that have been discussed.

SYSTEMATIC COMMUNICATION

In order to achieve the purposes of task-centered casework, the practitioner's communications need to be systematic. We use the term as a shorthand expression of a more complex notion, which we will attempt to clarify. Our model is designed to be carried out in a step-wise progression: the client's problems are explored, a target problem is identified, a task is formulated, durational limits are set, work on the task is carried out, and termination is effected. The practitioner is expected to concentrate his efforts on completing a particular step before moving on to the next. To the extent that he does, his communication is systematic in our sense of the term. A measure of this characteristic may be obtained by determining the proportion of the caseworker's communication that is directly relevant to completing the step at hand. For example, after a target problem has been identified, the practitioner's communications should be focused on task formulation. The systematic character of his communication is lessened if during this step he becomes engaged in a reexploration of the client's overall problem situation.

Although systematic communication must generally be focused upon relevant themes, more is meant by the notion than a simple lack of scatter in the caseworker's inputs. Systematic communication consists of caseworker responses which can logically be expected to further completion of the step being worked on. Thus a focused exploration of a possible target problem is not enough. The caseworker must attempt to move with the client toward a definition of the problem as the one to which their attention will be directed.

Contrasting levels of this quality may be illustrated by the following situation. Suppose the client's task is to become more consistent in enforcing rules for her children's behavior. She also has some problems in her marriage, but she and the caseworker agree at the outset that the focus of their work is to be on her relationship with the children. Nonetheless, she brings up her marital problems from time to time. If the caseworker freely permits discussion of these problems or stimulates further revelations of them through expressions of interest or active inquiry, we would regard his pattern of communication as relatively unsystematic in that respect. His communication might be considered relatively systematic if he allowed limited discussion of these problems but then brought the client back to work on the task. His communications would be judged to be highly systematic if he kept the focus of discussion quite strictly to the client's relationship with her children, permitting little if any talk of her marital difficulties.

In short-term treatment models such as ours the caseworker's efforts need to be relatively systematic since only a limited amount of time is available. Probably more can be efficiently accomplished if his communications are concentrated on achieving particular objectives at particular times. In addition, an orderly approach helps the client understand more fully the nature of treatment and his role in it.

Certain negative effects would probably result, however, if this principle were carried to an extreme; that is, if the practitioner were so determined to maintain focus upon the step at hand that he would not explore critical new problems or examine alternative tasks if the original task proved questionable. While practitioner communication in task-centered casework is considerably more systematic than in standard practice, it does not necessarily follow that the need to maintain focus overrides all other considerations. As we shall see shortly the second quality of practitioner communication in fact provides constraints against excessive focusing.

The risk of the practitioner's communication becoming too restrictive can be exaggerated. Systematic communication is not easy to achieve even when the practitioner is strongly committed to it. An emotionally distraught person swamped with a variety of problems may be in no position to move in an orderly, progressive fashion through the various steps of the model. Target problems and tasks are often not fully clarified in the initial phase and need further attention in subsequent phases; latent problems may emerge, new problems may develop, the client's talk may drift to other subjects as work on the tasks becomes difficult, and so on. Such complications place natural limits on the extent to which communication can be made systematic.

RESPONSIVE COMMUNICATION

The practitioner's communications might be highly systematic yet at the same time oblivious to the client's immediate perceptions and feelings. A well-organized pursuit of certain objectives may be necessary in short-term work but will accomplish little if it is carried out in a manner that the client finds deprecating or insensitive. Thus we ask the practitioner not only to be systematic but also *responsive* in his communications with clients.

In general, responsive communication provides the client with the kind of feedback that encourages his self-expression, helps him feel accepted and understood, and enables him to comprehend and make use of the caseworker's input. Specifically we consider the caseworker's communication to be responsive to the extent that it: 1) expresses interest in the client's communications and recognition of their value; 2) conveys empathic understanding, that is, comprehension and appreciation of the central meanings of the client's verbal and nonverbal messages; 3) builds upon the client's own communications.

Although a formal measure of responsiveness has not yet

been perfected, preliminary work suggests a measure of this variable can be based on a combination of these three components. Scales for each of these dimensions can be applied to segments of practitioner communication and then can be combined to yield an overall responsiveness rating. The measure is seen as molar (based on patterns of worker communication within an interview) rather than as molecular (based on individual responses). At present we have no way of knowing precisely how responsive a caseworker's communication must be to meet the requirements of the model. Very high levels of responsiveness may be difficult to maintain if communication is also to be systematic, a dilemma that we shall return to shortly.

Thus far, our efforts have been limited largely to an attempt to clarify and operationalize the construct. The first component, which consists of letting the client know his communications are of interest and value, is perhaps a first step for the two remaining components. A caseworker can take this step and go no further, but it would be difficult for him to show empathic understanding and build on the client's communication without showing an interest in, and respect for, the client's contributions.

This initial step requires attentive listening (which may be expressed as a form of nonverbal communication) and responding with vocal qualities and facial expressions which convey interest and receptivity. The caseworker need not agree with the content of the client's communication in order to be responsive at this level but he must, in one way or another, convey recognition of the value of the client's communication. The caseworker does not react with boredom, indifference, or does not dismiss as of little consequence what the client has expressed. Responding to the content of the client's communication with relevant questions or comments is certainly one indication of this aspect of responsiveness. On the other hand, tangential responses on the part of the caseworker, his introducing new subject matter, suggesting that the client talk of something else, or interpreting the client's communications as evasions or resistance would all amount to lack of responsiveness at this level.

Perhaps the most critical component of responsiveness is the communication of empathic understanding. A number of writers both in and out of the literature on interpersonal treatment have attempted to elucidate the hazy, but important, concept of empathy; a diversity of interpretations has been the result. Our usage of the term is close to that of Truax (1967):

Accurate empathy involves more than just the ability of the therapist to sense the patient's "private world" as if it were his own. It also involves more than just the ability of the therapist to know what the patient means. Accurate empathy involves both the sensitivity to current feelings and the verbal facility to communicate this understanding in a language attuned to the client's current feelings. . . . At a high level of accurate empathy the message "I am with you," is unmistakably clear . . . the therapist's remarks fit in just right with the client's mood and intent. (p. 555)

In view of the impressive theoretical and empirical work done by Truax, Carkhuff, and others on this particular concept of empathy, we have been tempted to borrow it more or less in its totality. We have not for at least two reasons. The main one is that this view of empathy has been developed within the tradition of Rogerian client-centered counseling, with its emphasis on the practitioner's reflecting back the client's communication to stimulate his exploration of his own thoughts, feelings, and experience. Thus the communication of empathy is defined in terms of Rogerian technique. If a practitioner does not rely heavily on some form of "reflecting back," then this notion of empathy, at least as it has been specified by Truax, becomes difficult to apply. The other reason is related to the first but involves certain technical considerations. Truax's conception of empathy is both complex and, at points, rather fuzzy. It has a number of dimensions, including the extent to which the therapist communicates awareness of "the most deeply shrouded of the client's feeling areas," and "meanings in the client's experience of which the client is scarcely aware." Such intricate and slippery indications of empathy may have some rationale within the client-centered framework, but their value becomes questionable when empathy is used in other contexts.

Our concept of empathy stresses the importance of conveying understanding and appreciation of the client's own interpretation of his world, but it does not require the practitioner to express his recognition of "what it must be like," in so many words. For example, let us suppose that a client has related an incident in which her husband, in front of guests, made a witty but possibly invidious remark about her behavior. One can think of any number of unempathic responses to the client, such as a comment on her husband's cleverness or an inquiry about the behavior that precipitated his remark. A more empathic kind of response would convey some recognition of her possible feelings about the incident, her irritation, embarrassment, or whatever. A practitioner might attempt to put these feelings into words, which would be one way of expressing empathy. An equally, if not more empathic response, in our view, might well be an inquiry about her reaction. The inquiry itself could serve as a way of conveying understanding and appreciation of what the incident may have meant to her, without risk of reading in "feelings" that she may not have had. While in many circumstances, the most appropriate way to express empathic understanding would be through some re-statement of the client's feelings and experiences, one would not see this form of expression as necessarily highest on the scale.

Empathic understanding is conveyed through nonverbal as well as verbal elements, usually with both contributing. A caseworker who says, "It's a tough decision" (in response to the client's presentation of a painful dilemma that must be re-solved) might express this rather slowly and softly, with his voice reflecting some of the tension that the client might be feeling. The caseworker's vocal expression would be an inte-gral part of conveying his recognition of what the client was experiencing. His message to the client would have quite a dif-ferent *meaning* if his response had been delivered in a brisk, hurried manner.

The third aspect of responsiveness concerns the extent to which the practitioner's responses build on the client's com-munications. Responsive communication not only conveys in-terest and understanding but also attempts to expand, amplify, and clarify the client's meanings.

One characteristic of communication about complex human problems and behavior is its incompleteness. A client remarks that he has been "feeling low." The message conveys a certain meaning but at the same time points to a larger ter-rain full of unknowns. In response to the practitioner's inqui-ries he may reveal he has been feeling depressed about his fi-nancial problems. A portion of the original terrain has been filled in but another has been opened up—what are his financial problems and how have they made him depressed? In this way communication about such matters proceeds: as new ground is covered, new horizons are revealed. Responsive communication on the practitioner's part addresses itself to the incompleteness of the client's meanings. If he is responsive, the practitioner stays within the frame of reference suggested by the client's message but attempts to help the client fill out this frame. The practitioner's response moves the client toward fuller expression of important thoughts and feelings at the edge of his immediate awareness.

An example may help to clarify this aspect of responsive communication. Suppose a client remarks to her caseworker that one of her children gave her a difficult time the day before. The caseworker can react unresponsively by letting the remark pass, by making some "appropriate" comment and changing the subject, or the like. A responsive reply might be to ask what happened. The client might then describe the particular difficulties she encountered—perhaps her child had been disobedient. The caseworker might ask questions or make comments that would enable the client to provide a fuller picture of the incident. But responsive communication is not simply confined to inquiries. The client might express uncertainty about the best way of handling such a problem. The caseworker might reply with a suggestion about what she might try or might comment on her general tendency to feel insecure in handling such problems (if such were the case). But if he were to do either in a responsive way he would shape his reply to the client's definition of her situation. At the same time he would introduce meanings related to, but different from, what the client had expressed. In so doing he would be giving the client a message she would be able to understand and take into account, yet one that would enhance her awareness of either possibilities for action or her response patterns.

This aspect of responsiveness differs from empathic understanding, although the two aspects are related. A message may convey empathy ("You seem quite upset over this") without adding much to the meaning the client has already expressed. Building on the client's communication normally conveys a certain amount of empathic understanding, but this is not always the case. The caseworker could add to the client's meanings without showing much appreciation for them.

EMPIRICAL AND THEORETICAL BASES

A good deal of evidence suggests there is a strong relationship between the practitioner's use of communication which we would call "responsive" and positive therapeutic outcomes. Much of the relevant empirical work has been concerned with the role of empathy in treatment. Since empathic communication is a central component of responsiveness, research on empathy is quite germane to our purpose.

In their review of research on "therapist interpersonal skills," Truax and Mitchell (1971) summarize the results of thirteen studies reporting "findings on the therapeutic effectiveness of accurate empathy." In nine of the studies, hypotheses predicting positive association between levels of empathy and outcome (overall, combined measures) were supported ($p < .05$). There were no significant findings counter to this type of hypothesis in any of the studies.

This body of research has its limitations. A single investigator (Truax) using one conception of empathy has been responsible for most of it. A more serious drawback is the lack of studies using experimental designs; thus it is not possible to say for sure that empathy is the effective variable. An alternative explanation is that the client who is likely to do well tends to draw forth empathic responses from the practitioner. While Truax and Mitchell (1971) present evidence that the therapist's empathy level is not determined by the patient, studies by Carkhuff and Alexik (1967) and Friel, Kratchovil, and Carkhuff (1968) demonstrate that clients can affect the levels of "low empathy" practitioners. Thus the question of causation remains unresolved, although the weight of evidence seems to be on the side of the hypothesis that the therapist level of empathy (in the Truax sense) does influence treatment outcome. Given the degree of overlap between our conception of responsiveness and Truax's measure of empathy, these findings also suggest that a high level of responsive communication may contribute to successful application of the present model.

Unfortunately, we cannot pinpoint why such factors as empathy or responsiveness may lead to positive changes in the client. We assume that if the client feels understood by the practitioner, then he is more willing to reveal his thoughts and feelings and more likely to feel secure and trusting in the treatment relationship. He may come to a quicker and fuller understanding of his problems and himself and may place more value on the practitioner's formulations. His being understood by another person whom he respects may be a "corrective" for earlier, more negative experiences, hence he may come to view others and himself in a more favorable light.

In addition, efforts to understand the client in an empathic way may influence certain qualities in the practitioner which in turn may help the course of effective treatment. As Truax and Carkhuff (1967) suggest: "As we come to know [the client] from his personal vantage point we automatically come to value and like him. Perhaps precisely because we are concentrating on *his* experience, we are much freer from everyday threat and insecurity and so can be in those moments more genuine and authentic" (p. 42).

In general, responsive communication is another expression of our emphasis upon the phenomenological world of the client. The model is addressed to the problems he perceives and attempts to help him carry out actions that make sense to him. To carry out the model, the practitioner must steer close to the informational system that guides the client's thoughts and behavior. To help this system function more effectively, the practitioner constantly must be in tune with the meanings and manners of the client's communications.

If the caseworker is responsive in this sense, he may at least be able to avoid or minimize the many kinds of miscommunications that can occur between him and the client. From studies by Mayer and Timms (1970) and Silverman (1970), we have gained a detailed picture of the communications problem that arises when caseworkers attempt to impose their thought-ways upon working-class clients. In order to help clients of any class the caseworker needs, as we see it, to comprehend and work within the client's own mode of construing reality.

RESPONSIVE VERSUS SYSTEMATIC
COMMUNICATION

The theoretical considerations and empirical evidence just presented have lead us to conclude that a high level of responsiveness should characterize the communication of practitioners using the present model. At present, this requirement must remain vague, since we have not yet developed criteria to determine how much responsiveness is required to achieve a high level. We would certainly not expect all practitioner responses to attain this level, whatever it might be. We would anticipate considerable variation in this quality within the life of a case and even within an interview. We expect, however, that the bulk of the practitioner's communication would fall on the upper side of both an overall measure of this quality and of measures of its three dimensions.

The simultaneous requirement that communication be systematic might well be the single greatest constraint on the practitioner's responsiveness. Conceivably his communication could be both maximally systematic and responsive, but this condition would require an extraordinarily well-focused client. Considerable scatter and drift are natural characteristics of the communication of troubled people. If the caseworker were to push responsiveness to the limit he could scarcely maintain the requirement to be systematic with a client who would lead him up hills and down valleys. To put the point in concrete form, if a client whose task concerned her relationship with her mother switched off into a recounting of a quarrel with her boy friend, the caseworker would be faced with a dilemma. If he were to react responsively, he would move naturally into a discussion of the quarrel and away from the task. If he were to be systematic he would try to bring the client back to the task with a loss of responsiveness.

There is no ideal resolution to this paradox. The case-worker usually cannot be *both* completely responsive and systematic. He must balance the one requirement against the other, but still he should be able to achieve at least a moderately high level on both qualities in most cases.

There are perhaps ways of communicating that preserve both qualities. A practitioner can be selective in his responsiveness; that is, he can give greater attention to client communications that are likely to further accomplishment of the step at hand. He can convey empathic understanding and appreciation of tangential difficulties the client may be facing but still insist that they return to the target problem or task. If the client has agreed to a certain plan of work then he is more likely to comprehend and accept the caseworker's efforts to bring him back to it, and less likely to interpret these efforts as an expression of lack of interest in his problems. Through these means the client may be helped to learn how to communicate more systematically so that the caseworker can be more fully and naturally responsive within the limits of an agreed-upon structure.

But many uncertainties remain. Usually the caseworker is unsure about how best to accomplish a given treatment step, hence it is often difficult to know when communication is becoming unsystematic, and there always lurks the possibility that the agreed-upon focus of work was not wisely chosen or is no longer valid. There is always a question about how far a practitioner should go in being responsive in an area that is peripheral to the treatment plan yet still of immediate concern to the client. We know very little of the precise consequences that follow from a sacrifice of systematic communication for the sake of responsiveness and vice versa. These are some of the quandaries with which we must be concerned in further work on the model.

THE TREATMENT "RELATIONSHIP"

What we have said about qualities of the practitioner's communication might have been expressed, as such matters often are, under the rubric of the treatment "relationship." The term has limited use in our vocabulary, for in our opinion it is a word whose usefulness has been fatally impaired by the variety of vague and ambiguous meanings that it has accrued in over a half-century of treatment literature. "Relationship" may be used to describe the sum total of events that occur between practitioner and client; or it may refer to certain qualities of these interactions, particularly of the attitudinal and emotional variety. Sometimes its referent is some kind of "meaningful" interaction, as in the old saw, "It takes time to establish a relationship with a client." The list could easily be extended. In any of these contexts the term is used to refer to critical factors. The problem with it is that one is never sure which critical factors are being denoted.

The events of treatment may be described, and we think with greater clarity, without recourse to this overused construct. In our system specified aspects of practitioner and client communication are employed as the means of conceptualizing at least some of the important referents of "relationship." Although we have as yet specified only certain of the complex elements that characterize practitioner-client communication, we would rather be relatively clear about parts of the whole than nebulous about the whole itself.

CHAPTER SEVEN

BASIC STRATEGY AND TECHNIQUES

BEFORE WE present a range of methods the caseworker may use to further the client's task achievement we want to place these methods in the context of contemporary practice. The treatment strategies currently specified in the model are derived largely from what might be called "standard professional casework practice," the kind of casework that is carried on by most graduate caseworkers in most settings and that is taught in most schools of social work. It is the kind of practice that has been elucidated by such writers as Gordon Hamilton (1951) and Florence Hollis (1964).

SOME OBSERVATIONS
ON CASEWORK METHODS

As a result of the strong influence of psychoanalytic treatment theories, prevailing modes of casework rely heavily upon techniques designed to bring about change in the client's cognitions. As several studies of casework have indicated (Reid, 1967; Hollis, 1968; Mullen, 1968; Pinkus, 1968), the bulk of the caseworker's communication characterized by any kind of demonstrable change-goal is directed at helping the client increase his understanding of others, his interaction with others, and his own behavior. Most of the caseworker's communications that do not fall into these categories appear to consist of explorations, mostly inquiries, into the client's problems, behavior, feelings, current situation, and earlier history. Much of this exploratory activity seems directed at laying the groundwork for comments, interpretations, formulations, and the like about the client and his milieu. Often the caseworker's inquiries themselves, particularly leading or focused questions, are designed to stimulate the client's thinking in ways that might lead to an increase in his understanding, although sometimes exploration may be used primarily as a means of helping the client to "get things off his chest." To this array of methods can be added advice-giving and reassurance, normally used to a rather limited extent. These methods are usually seen as being most effective when used in a sustained relationship in which the caseworker presents himself as a warm, understanding, and tolerant person. This relationship itself is viewed as having therapeutic benefits. The client may change in constructive directions because of his positive experience with an empathic and accepting practitioner and he may learn to correct dysfunctional modes of responding to others by gaining insight into unrealistic aspects of his relationship with the caseworker.

In most settings this form of interpersonal or "talking" treatment is carried on through weekly interviews. Many of the problems caseworkers deal with, however, require a good deal of work with persons other than the client—with physicians, relatives, foster parents, teachers, judges, other social workers, and so on. These efforts, which vary in amount and nature from setting to setting have always been very much a part of casework practice. In work with some clients— families in need of multiple services for example—the caseworker's interventions in the client's milieu may be the central focus of his activity. Such interventions are usually viewed, however, as ancillary to interviews with the client.

Certain common modes of practice, such as family group treatment, crisis-intervention, and Perlman's problem-solving approach, do depart, of course, from the kind of standard casework practice we have described, but they can be more accurately described as variants of standard practice than true alternatives. Family members may be seen together, the focus may be on a particular crisis, or treatment may be conducted within a problem-solving framework but still one finds the same stress on the values of cognitive change and relationship, to name two central common denominators. Such similarities have become more apparent since the recent emergence of a radically different form of treatment, namely behavior modification.

The caseworker operations set forth in our approach have also evolved from psychoanalytically oriented casework practice. Graduate caseworkers should be already familiar with the array of direct and indirect interventions we offer, although they may find our application of them novel in a number of respects.

THE QUESTION OF EFFECTIVENESS. We have chosen these methods because we know them best and not because we have conclusive evidence that they are effective. While we have presented a good empirical case for the proposition that the yield of these methods is as great in short-term as in long-term treatment contexts, we have no way of proving that they are more efficacious than some other set of methods or indeed that they accomplish any thing more than clients could on their own.

On the other hand, it would be premature to write off the heavy investment that has been made in contemporary case-work methodology on the basis of existing evidence. It is true that casework as we have described it has failed to achieve predicted effects in a number of experiments, but for the most part these studies have tested casework treatment of clients who did not initiate service and who perhaps did not want it (Powers and Witmer, 1951; Meyer, Borgatta, and Jones, 1964; Wallace, 1967; Mullen, Chazin and Feldstein, 1970). More-over, the goals of the casework services tested in these experiments were, in our judgment, excessively diffuse and overambitious—to prevent delinquent behavior, to enhance academic achievement in general, to foster personality development, to help families become financially independent, and so forth. These studies have been useful in telling us what casework cannot be expected to accomplish and in stimulating efforts to discover what it can. As Briar (1971) has said: "the problem posed for casework by these studies is how to increase its effectiveness" (p. 125).

The potential efficacy of the methods used by most caseworkers—and those advocated in our model—need to be evaluated in light of accumulated evidence on the effectiveness of similar forms of interpersonal treatment. Two comprehensive reviews of research on the effectiveness of psychotherapy (Meltzoff and Kornreich, 1970; Bergin, 1971) conclude that conventional forms of psychotherapy have been able to demonstrate measurable degrees of effectiveness. These are conclusions based upon review of a large number of experimental studies in which the progress of patients or clients who have received treatment have been compared against the progress of individuals who did not. While not all such experiments have shown that interpersonal treatment is effective, a substantial number do. After considering the manifold problems involved in such reviews, Bergin (1971) concludes:

. . . there remains some modest evidence that psychotherapy works. While most studies do not seem to yield very substantial evidence that this is so, the number that do appear to be larger than would be expected by chance; therefore, something potent or efficacious must be operating in some portion of the therapy that is routinely done, even though average effects are only moderately impressive when diverse cases, therapists and change scores are lumped together. (p. 229)

Although some reviewers (Eysenck, 1966; Truax and Carkhuff, 1967) have come to conclusions less favorable to psychotherapy, there seems to have accumulated a group of well-designed studies that have at least demonstrated that practitioners can bring about change in psychological and social problems through communicative processes. Unfortunately these studies do not offer a basis for any generalizations about why treatment may have been effective.

The challenge to the model-builder is then to discover ways in which the effectiveness of treatment can be maximized. Outcome research on psychotherapy and casework perhaps does offer some directions. Elsewhere in his review, Bergin (1971) makes a strong case that treatment may result in deterioration. While a number of studies show no differences in average changes between treated and untreated groups, treated groups in these studies have more variable outcomes—that is, higher proportions of treatment recipients both get better and get worse than their untreated counterparts. Although it is not clear what may be responsible for such a "deterioration effect," Bergin suggests that among recipients who deteriorate are "those who have already obtained a neurotic equilibrium that is upset by the therapist, resulting in a new cycle of deterioration" (p. 248). This hypothesis receives support from the Reid and Shyne study (1969): clients receiving an average of eight months of service (extended treatment) showed more deterioration than clients receiving four months of service. Since clients in both groups were treated by the same caseworkers, the differences cannot be explained by variation in the competence of the practitioners. Quite possibly, treatment carried beyond certain limits not only may yield diminishing returns but it may also have deleterious effects by upsetting the equilibrium the client may have achieved with help of treatment up to that point or with the passage of time.

With this in mind, it is instructive to examine the studies that form the principal base for the conclusion of Meltzoff and Kornreich (1970) that the effectiveness of psychotherapy has been amply demonstrated by published research. They base this conclusion upon a number of studies with designs they consider "adequate" (generally experimental) and outcomes they deem "positive" (that is, revealing greater change for treated than untreated patients). If we restrict ourselves to studies of individual treatment using conventional methods of interpersonal influence (eliminating studies of group treatment, behavior modification, and hypnotherapy) we find in this review some seventeen studies with adequate designs and positive results. Since the treated groups did better on the average than untreated groups, we assume that treatment was relatively free of deterioration effects. In almost half these studies the course of treatment was completed in less than four months, and the median length for all courses of treatment in the seventeen studies was six months. Although deterioration effects have been identified in brief treatment (Bergin, 1971), it may well be that such effects are less likely to occur in treatment that ends prior to or shortly after initial reequilibration.

The very fact that treatment appears capable of producing deleterious effects strengthens the case for brief treatment designs. If the explanation we have offered is valid, then we would want to limit the duration of treatment to avoid disturbing restitutive mechanisms. If therapist incompetence is the cause, then limitations on the length of service may protect clients from exposure to protracted ineptitude. Until we know more about the incidence and causes of negative therapeutic effects, some restrictions on the amount of "help" we dose out may be advisable.

Although traditional methods of psychotherapy and casework may be effective under certain conditions, we are hard put to find ways to improve upon the effectiveness of these methods unless we can begin to specify those conditions. We have made little progress toward this end despite thousands of articles and studies concerned in one way or another with this kind of specification. One reason so little headway has been made lies in the nature of the phenomenon under investigation—interpersonal treatment itself. Conventional methods of casework and psychotherapy do not lend themselves very well either to systematic study or to development through research. Their goals tend to be poorly formulated, global and diffuse; their processes, complex to begin with, become increasingly entangled as they operate over lengthy periods of time. If one assumes that empirical research is our most powerful means for improving treatment, priority should be given to constructing treatment models that can be improved through research. Such models would need to be addressed to specific goals from which precise, measurable outcome criteria could be derived. These techniques would need to be explicitly stated and capable of being defined at operational levels. Almost of necessity, courses of treatment would need to be brief, not only to enable adequate study of processes but to permit the rapid feedback of research results into model development.

In sum, outcome research on conventional methods of treatment offers some rationale for their use in new models of intervention but only with the provision that systematic efforts be made to improve their effectiveness. There is good reason to believe that short-term designs directed at specific goals and capable of development through research may be a way forward. We hope that brief, task-centered casework is an example of this kind of treatment approach.

THE BASIC STRATEGY OF
TASK-CENTERED CASEWORK

The basic strategy of brief, task-centered casework rests on one central assumption: that the effectiveness and efficiency of methods normally used in casework practice can be increased considerably if they are concentrated on helping clients achieve specific and limited goals of their own choice within brief, bounded periods of service. We are not advocating a new technology, but rather a restructuring of the technology we already have. Is this merely old wine in new bottles? We think not. A more appropriate metaphor might be the difference between light diffused through a fog and light focused through a lens. Coming to terms with the client on what he wants to pursue is perhaps half the strategy. More than in normal practice, the caseworker concentrates his efforts on identifying and pinning down what the client wants to do and how he can do it. The client's commitment to the task is crucial; the client must say in effect, "This is what I am willing to try to achieve." In order to help him get to that point, the caseworker may need to apply his techniques to enable the client to clarify his goals, to appraise his resources, to recognize that he must make a choice between action and inaction, and to decide on a course of action to take.

Once a task is agreed upon, the caseworker's techniques are concentrated almost exclusively on helping the client carry it out. It is assumed that this focusing of activity is one key to the relative success of brief, time-limited therapies. Not only is a maximum of caseworker effort brought to bear upon a narrow sector of the client's life-space, but the client's efforts are concentrated there as well. In this context obstacles to change in the client's behavior or situation are thrown into sharp relief and can be more effectively dealt with. The mobilizing pressures of time limits operating upon both caseworker and client—perhaps another key to the success of brief treatment —serves to push both toward task achievement.

In most cases the client agrees to take immediate action to solve his problem. The caseworker's strategy is aimed at helping him carry out that action. We assume that people can usually alter their behavior or undertake new behavior rather quickly if they have a clear idea of what they are to do and want to do it. The caseworker's role is to encourage and guide these behaviors and to help the client achieve whatever understanding he may need to carry them out. Thus, in task-centered casework a mother who has some recognition that she overprotects her son (but "can't help it") is not asked to consider why she has this need but rather assumes the task of giving him greater independence in particular ways. Her own striving, guided and encouraged by the caseworker, may well be enough to enable her to become less overprotective. If she cannot, then the question of why not, is taken up, but only in relation to her efforts to achieve specific, agreed-upon changes.

Pursuit of this strategy entails certain risks and sacrifices. Choices must be made and, if at all possible, adhered to. The choices may be in error. Since the focus of attention is narrow, the client must be expected to tend to various problems on his own. He may not be able to use the caseworker as an all-purpose helper or confidant if anything substantial is to be accomplished. We think, however, that the risks and sacrifices can be justified by what can be achieved.

These elements of strategy define the model and are essential to its operation. We are less sure about the techniques we suggest be used to implement the strategy. Since they have unproven efficacy, we cannot insist that practitioners who use our model restrict themselves to them. Moreover, the approaches we will presently spell out do not begin to cover the range of possible methods that may be used within the framework of the model.

The practitioner is free, therefore, to use whatever means he judges to be the most effective in helping the client carry out the task; more than that he should be continually in search of better methods of task accomplishment than those we offer. As we have suggested in various ways, task-centered casework is certainly not a self-sufficient system of treatment. At its present state of development, its chief contribution may well be to provide a structure for the practitioner's treatment activities, whatever their sources and characteristics.

TYPES OF CASEWORKER COMMUNICATION

In the preceding chapter we presented a communications framework for the caseworker's activities in the present model. Certain *general qualities* of the caseworker's communications were considered, that is, qualities which can be used to characterize any of his communications. We now turn to different *types* of communications used by the caseworker in his application of the model. Since each type has distinctive characteristics and functions, each may be referred to as a technique or method of treatment. Five categories have been identified: exploration, structuring, enhancing awareness, encouragement, and direction. These techniques will be examined largely as they are used to help clients carry out tasks, but attention will also be given to their applications in prior steps of the model. After discussing how each method may be employed in direct work with clients, we will consider their use in communications with individuals other than clients.

EXPLORATION. Exploration is a method basic to all models of interpersonal treatment. As used here, the term refers to the practitioner's efforts to elicit data from the client. It serves two purposes: to provide the worker with needed information and to focus the flow of communication on relevant content. Although exploration may stimulate change, through conveying the practitioner's expectations for example, it is not primarily directed toward effecting change.

In the present model, exploration is directed initially to eliciting and clarifying the client's problems and examining task possibilities. Once a task has been formulated, exploration is concentrated primarily on task-related questions: what efforts has the client made toward carrying out the task? what has he accomplished? what difficulties is he encountering? how is he trying to overcome them? and so on. Data gathered on the client's task performance through exploration provides the informational basis for the practitioner's operations in all subsequent categories.

In task-centered casework, exploration is not generally used, as it often is in other approaches, to investigate client concerns unrelated to the task focus. The caseworker normally will try to steer clear of problem areas in the client's life other than those that reasonably can be construed to fall within the agreed-upon focus of work. This proscription should not restrain the caseworker from being responsive or from lending a sympathetic ear to concerns not related to the task, but he does not normally explore them or encourage the client to stay with them.

For example, the young man whose treatment task was to raise his work efficiency brought up his concern about his relationship with his girl friend who might be pregnant. It was known that this young man engaged in casual affairs which frequently led him into difficult situations. It was understood that he had problems of many sorts in his peer relationships.

Nevertheless, because he was in treatment to achieve an important goal of raising his work efficiency, the concern he expressed about his girl friend's condition was not explored in depth. The principal exception to this rule occurs when the "peripheral" problem appears to be of such overriding concern to the client that a shift in the target problem and the resulting task may seem indicated.

STRUCTURING. Structuring operations comprise the worker's communications *about* the structure and direction of his interactions with the client. They include general explanations of the purpose and nature of treatment, which are given at the beginning of treatment but may need reexpression during its course; communications about the problem, tasks, and time limits around which treatment will be organized; and specific focusing responses which explicitly direct the flow of client communication toward task-relevant content.

There is evidence to suggest that many clients, particularly the less well educated, have difficulty grasping the purposes and nature of "talking" treatment and that client misunderstandings of what the practitioner is about can contribute to poor results. At least one study (Hoehn-Saric et al., 1964) has indicated that efforts to orient lower-class patients to what they might expect and what might be expected of them in psychotherapy leads to better outcomes.

Clients receiving brief task-centered casework should be given to understand, in principle and through examples, that treatment will be aimed at helping them toward a resolution of specific problems they are most concerned about, that they will be expected to take specific action with the caseworker's assistance to alleviate such problems, and that the course of treatment will be confined to certain limits. Since the client's cooperation is an obvious requirement for successful case-work, and since he can cooperate better if he knows what the caseworker and he are supposed to do, one wonders why more emphasis has not been placed on fairly full explanations of treatment. Perhaps one reason is that the objectives and structure of traditional forms of casework are rather difficult to communicate. Because of its more limited goals and tighter structure, this model, as well as short-term treatment approaches generally, are more readily interpreted and understood.

The second aspect of structuring consists of the worker's efforts to shape the specific treatment plan for his client. The worker uses exploration to obtain an understanding of what the client perceives as his problems or potential tasks. From this base he makes whatever inputs are necessary to reach agreements with the client, first on the target problem, then on the task to be undertaken to alleviate the problem and finally on the duration and organization of treatment. Structuring of this type is used most heavily in the initial interviews but is also employed subsequently to help the client clarify and specify the task to be pursued, the durational limits, or other aspects of treatment structure. Or in some cases much of the initial structuring process may need to be repeated if emerging problems or shifts in the client's motivations result in need to replace the original tasks.

The caseworker's statements made about projected treatment strategy need not be detailed, because this kind of planning cannot be done ahead of time in any treatment process. In fact, care should be taken to avoid too fully detailed a plan in order to retain necessary flexibility and avoid becoming locked into procedures which need to be changed to accomplish the task. These plans, however, should be made explicit in at least a general manner. For example, with Mr. Todd, the client whose task was "to raise his efficiency level at work," it was agreed that the weekly interviews in his course of treatment would concentrate upon overcoming his tendencies to give priority to distractions. This client had already identified that "distractability" was the enemy of his work productivity. The client considered this "agenda" and agreed to it. He was also advised that when this agenda appeared unproductive or if he should change his mind, the proposal along with the task would be planfully reviewed and altered as necessary.

The third part of the caseworker's structuring operations —providing explicit guides for the client's communication— is made easier if the first two parts have been successfully carried out. For example, focusing operations may be less necessary if the client understands that treatment as a whole is to concentrate on a specific problem and is clear about what this problem is. Still the caseworker will need to provide some direction for the client—certainly more so than in conventional casework. Some of this direction, as has been noted, is supplied implicitly through exploration—by asking certain questions and not others. In structuring, the practitioner's directives are more explicit, "Perhaps one should stick with this problem," or "Let's go back to a point you made earlier." Structuring at this level is used primarily to maintain the focus of communication on agreed-upon tasks.

It may be, however, that a new or old problem of living may emerge with sufficient force to knock out the client's motivation to work on the task. It may overshadow the initial problem rendering it relatively unimportant by comparison. This kind of situation may call for a reformulation of the task as the caseworker and client turn their attention to the emerging difficulties in a systematic manner. It is obviously important to attempt to distinguish between passing or peripheral concerns, concerns of long standing about which little can be done, and emergent problems requiring a shift in the task. This distinction is often difficult to make and we have no precise criteria by which to determine the difference. The rule of thumb which has been found to be useful is for the caseworker to discuss with the client what the course ought to be. This is best accomplished by reviewing what the task agreement was, by offering the reminder that at the time it was undertaken a decision was made with care and thought, that it was then seriously considered to be of a high order of importance. The caseworker then asks the client to consider whether that level of importance still pertains, and if not, why not? Thus it may often be possible to secure information which can assist both client and caseworker in deciding whether or not to depart from the task. Finally there may arise urgent and time-limited occurrences which must be immediately dealt with and where doing so preserves the ability of client and caseworker to proceed and take up the task again as soon as possible.

The importance of structuring in task-centered work can hardly be overemphasized. Operations of this kind have not been given too much stress in standard casework practice since treatment goals tend to be sufficiently broad or elastic to incorporate most foci that may arise. Moreover, there is adequate time—or at least the expectation that there will be adequate time—to attend to a multiplicity of concerns. In the present model, as in planned brief approaches generally—the caseworker and client must make choices on foci that can determine the subsequent course of treatment. The task-centered caseworker may find the choices particularly difficult because of the general requirement of the model that the agreed-upon task be adhered to unless the client explicitly decides otherwise. In his efforts to hold the client to the task, the practitioner may feel he is blocking treatment from shifting naturally to problems of greater importance.

For an illustration of some of these observations, we will return to Mr. Todd, the young man who was underachieving at work, but this time will consider his case in its entirety. Mr. Todd thought that his poor work achievement was part of a lifelong pattern. Since the age of nine he had persistently underachieved in school, culminating in his dropping out of college in his junior year. Even though he was not failing, his grades were so much lower than he and his family expected that he was overwhelmed with hopelessness and dropped the whole endeavor. He thought that perhaps by taking some time away from school he might recover his spirits and find the courage to return to school later. From data obtained in the first two interviews it was clear that the distractions which prevented Mr. Todd from attending to his work were the same as those which had interfered with his school performance. A lonely young man with low self-esteem, he frittered away much of his work day in social contacts. But his socializing was not just play. He was using his friends and acquaintances "to find out what life was all about" and enjoyed offering them his guidance on their problems. All this was more important to Mr. Todd than work or study. Furthermore, when he did get down to work he was so anxious that he took on enormous quantities of detail which could just as well have been collapsed into a few jobs or ignored.

Under these circumstances, Mr. Todd persistently wondered in his sessions whether the treatment agenda could possibly intervene in such a burdensome tangle of issues by such apparently simplistic devices as setting himself a schedule, finding control devices he might use to bind his anxiety, concentrating upon his determination to achieve instead of spending his time in unproductive socializing. Mr. Todd consumed substantial quantities of interview time with these concerns about the propriety of the task to the point that the caseworker himself became skeptical about the effectiveness of such a regime. In addition, he brought up the difficulty he might be in if his girl friend proved to be pregnant, which was a possibility. Later it emerged that she was not but that he had moved into still another liaison which was repeating an old pattern. The new girl friend had quickly become dependent on him and he, as usual, was resentful about her demands and guilty about taking advantage of her. Another area opened up when Mr. Todd revealed that he was becoming closely involved with an older man at work, who was taking him under his wing. Although Mr. Todd was feeling satisfied and secure under the tutelage of this friendly older man, it seemed likely that he was repeating a pattern of overdependence upon paternal figures. The caseworker did not pursue these tangential themes, however.

Then, apparently as a reaction to the caseworker's firmness in attempting to maintain the agreed upon focus or formulate a change, Mr. Todd accused the caseworker of coldness and insensitivity. He did not see how he could improve his lot in such a climate. The caseworker, shriven with doubts, performed an act of faith in encouraging adherence to the task instead of taking up these complexities.

In the ninth, and next to last, interview Mr. Todd stated that he had come to a decision. His efficiency rating was to be made in two weeks but he was already informed it would be "very satisfactory," one level above what he had received the last time. Not getting an "excellent" or "superior" rating (of which he was capable) did not now loom as any great disaster. His father would disapprove of him but he was used to that. What had become clearer to him was how much he valued his personal relationships—with his older friend who would protect him, with his many friends at work and outside work with whom the hours spent offered him highly meaningful gratifications. His penchant for detail on his job might possibly turn into an asset, as his supervisor sought assignments for him where this quality had value.

He was no longer so fixed on returning to college. He thought he would let that issue slide for a time and see what emerged. He said that the caseworker's firmness with him in pursuing the task that he himself had devised had helped improve his performance at work. He appreciated that but had come to realize that other things were more important. By being closely held to examining this objective, he had learned that he did not value it as much as he had thought. Instead, what he valued most was what he had—a steady job, a level of achievement which was satisfactory to his employers, and a rich set of social relationships which he enjoyed and which offered him interpersonal rewards of a high order. He still thought he had a lot of problems to straighten out. He was acquiring comfort now in his relationships with women. He thought he could in the future attend to that area perhaps with therapy and perhaps not. How he might work on these problems was taken up in the last interview.

Not all tasks partake of the convolutions of this one. It was chosen to discuss here because in this one case most of the vicissitudes of the task are revealed. However, all tasks appear to have a natural life which contain elements of uncertainty and obscurity. It should be expected that the task must undergo an altered perception as its meaning unfolds by the very act of taking it seriously and working on it. This seems to be no more or less than the general idea that the solution to every problem gives rise to new ones. Perhaps the only question which needs answering is whether the new problem is more palatable than the old. With Mr. Todd that seems to have been the case.

CHANGE-ORIENTED TECHNIQUES

We now turn to what might be called "change-oriented" techniques. While exploration and structuring have latent and indirect change functions, their immediate purpose is to lay the ground work for methods that are more directly aimed at change. Awareness-enhancement, direction, and encouragement, on the other hand, are expressly designed to affect modification in the client's perception, attitudes, feelings, and actions. Essentially these techniques consist of messages the caseworker transmits to the client. The change intent is either apparent or can be readily inferred from an analysis of the message.

ENHANCING THE CLIENT'S AWARENESS. Techniques in this broad category normally constitute the bulk of the practitioner's change-oriented communications in the present model. They comprise the practitioner's efforts to provide the client with information about his own behavior and problems, about others, or about his situation. This information may range from facts about some novel situation that the client is facing to formulations about some aspect of his own behavior that he has not perceived. In this category are included operations which in other systems have such labels as "interpretation," "clarification," "confrontation," and "reflection." In our system these various types of interventions are grouped into two sub-categories: 1) responses aimed at increasing the client's awareness of others and his situation; 2) responses aimed at increasing the client's awareness of the nature and dynamics of his own behavior or of his interactions with others.

Among the more common responses in the first sub-category are practitioner statements about resources, about events the client is about to experience (such as hospitalization or surgery), about normative aspects of human behavior (such as developmental problems of adolescents), or about particular characteristics of individuals with whom the client is interacting. The dominant response types in the second sub-category consist of practitioner statements which call to the client's attention aspects of his behavior that may be causing him difficulty or problematic aspects of his interactions with others, including the effects his behavior may have on others.

This formulation of the practitioner's efforts to enhance the client's awareness is somewhat broader than usual conceptions of this sort which tend to be concerned largely with the client's insight into his own behavior. In our view, all practitioner inputs whose immediate function is to add to or affect the client's cognition about his world or himself are best regarded as falling in a single class. Efforts to develop the client's *self*-awareness are thus seen as a part of a larger strategy, rather than as a group of methods to be set aside in a special category. Also we have eliminated customary distinctions among types of techniques concerned with the development of self-awareness, for example, distinctions concerning whether the focus of attention is on the nature of the client's behavior as opposed to its causes, or is on its current manifestations as opposed to its developmental origins.

While our method of classification is a part of a theoretical rationale which will be developed subsequently, the point can be made here that it better fits the realities of casework practice than do typologies which isolate and refine techniques which concern the development of the client's self-awareness as such. In a method such as casework in which major attention is given to the client's interactions with his social field, it is difficult to parcel out those interventions concerned just with the client's awareness of self. Moreover, the studies of casework practice previously referred to suggest that only a relatively small proportion of the caseworker's interventions can be identified as attempts to contribute to the client's understanding of his own patterns of behavior and that various sub-categories of technique of this genre are not used with sufficient frequency to warrant special classification.

Operations to enhance awareness are concentrated on helping the client carry out specific tasks. In keeping with our principle that communication should be systematic, little value is attached to increasing the client's awareness of matters unrelated to the task, although awareness achieved in connection with the task may have benefits beyond accomplishing the task itself. Much of the caseworker's use of awareness-enhancing techniques occurs in helping the client work through *obstacles* to task achievement. By definition a task involves the client's carrying out some course of action, one which he usually finds difficult to execute since, presumably, it is addressed to a problem that he has been unable to solve. The ensuing difficulties may involve his own behavior, the behavior of others, or characteristics of his social situation. It is assumed that if the client can be helped to understand the nature and origin of these obstacles he will be better able to overcome them. Thus the client's task may involve achieving a greater degree of independence from her mother. Obstacles might include her inability to say "No" to unrealistic demands her mother may place upon her and her perception of her mother as a suffering person who needs her care. In helping the client work through these impediments to task achievement, the caseworker may try to help her become aware of her pattern of submissiveness to her mother's demands and to see her mother in a more realistic light.

Although carried out within a different framework, the work of Stein, Murdaugh, and McLeod (1969) demonstrates how awareness-enhancing techniques can be used in short-term treatment to resolve a particular kind of obstacle— "cognitive misconceptions" about physical illness. Such misconceptions, according to these authors, contribute in a central way to various kinds of disturbed reactions to illness.

Although a dynamic basis often exists for the fantasies and cognitive distortions, we generally do not explore or deal with these 'roots' of the misperceptions in short-term treatment but concentrate, rather, at the cognitive level. In working toward *cognitive mastery,* the important steps include, first, the gradual working through of denial, with heavy reliance on the therapeutic alliance, and second, gradual presentation of reality after the fantasies and cognitive distortions have been explored and clarified. The resulting improved cognitive perception of reality permits a more stress-free adaptation to be achieved. (p. 1046)

In our framework this specific approach might be used with clients whose tasks involved the alleviation of emotional distress precipitated by physical illness. More generally, helping the client to achieve "cognitive mastery" would be an important technique in any situation in which cognitive distortions constituted an obstacle to task achievement.

Obstacles to task achievement may arise or be revealed in the client's interactions with the caseworker. The client's work on the task may be blocked by certain feelings or attitudes he may have toward the caseworker. For example, a client might paint a distorted picture of his progress in order to please the caseworker or avoid his criticism or may delay taking necessary action on his problem because of a need to "hang-on" to his relationship with the caseworker, or the client's problem-solving efforts may be impeded by problems of response that can be observed in his behavior in the interview. A wife's submissiveness toward her husband may parallel her submissiveness toward the caseworker.

The caseworker attempts to help the client understand these reactions as a part of enabling him to become aware of, and to work through, obstacles standing in the way of the task. Analysis of such reactions, or transference phenomena to use the psychoanalytic expression, is limited to this purpose. (This point is illustrated in one of the cases discussed in chapter 11.)

In some situations, enhancing the client's awareness serves more to facilitate task behavior than to remove specific obstacles; for example, the caseworker provides a client who is seeking residential care with information about possible institutions. In others the task itself may require the client to increase his understanding, as in the example of the mother whose task was to gain a more accurate perception of her child's behavior. If so, use of techniques in this category provide the most direct means to task fulfillment.

It is always difficult to draw the line between awareness-enhancing that is task-relevant and that which is not. In order to be less domineering with her son, a mother may need to understand not only that she tends to be domineering in other interpersonal relationships, but why she has these tendencies. From this point it would be possible to fan out into innumerable facets of her personality functioning and etiology. To say that our interest is in helping her achieve only the insight necessary to bring about a change in her behavior toward her son does not tell us how far we have to go to enable her to gain that degree and quality of insight. The only guideline we can offer is a recommendation that the caseworker expressly relate whatever kind of awareness he may help the client develop back to the task. This should help both from getting too far afield and should also serve to concentrate the change forces stimulated by the client's awareness on one critical point—the task itself.

It is much easier to describe methods of increasing the client's awareness than to provide either a theoretical rationale for their use or evidence that they lead to changes in behavior. The notion that increased understanding of one's self and milieu can be a force for change has roots in psychoanalytic theory, in various theories of learning and in common observation.

As Urban and Ford (1971) point out, most systems of psychotherapy are based upon the assumption "that a person's overall behavioral organization is governed and regulated by his cognitive functions, amplified and attenuated by the emotional patterns that have become associated with them. . . .

Since it is assumed that a person's actions are judged by such subjective behaviors, it is anticipated that if the person can be brought to think and hence feel differently, he will necessarily come to act differently as well" (p. 18).

There is little doubt that increases in awareness can influence changes in behavior, as anyone who has used a road map can testify. Individuals in daily life, as well as clients, use information of various sorts as a basis for making decisions and guiding their actions. More at issue is what kind of understanding is needed when the behavior to be changed consists of habituated patterns of response that reflect the individual's needs and beliefs, and hence is relatively resistive to alteration. Unfortunately, much of the behavior that clients' need to change to accomplish tasks is of this sort. Clinicians know full well the limitations of insight of whatever form in bringing about modifications of such behavior, particularly behavior that contributes to problems of interpersonal conflict, role performance, and dissatisfactions in social relations.

We propose that the increases in the client's awareness of himself and his world can occur and contribute to change in his behavior when certain conditions are met. We expect that practitioners who use the model will attempt to bring about these conditions to the fullest extent possible.

Perhaps the fundamental condition is the client's willingness to change his behavior. For a mother to be interested in gaining new perspectives on her relationship with her child and to make use of the information, she must have some commitment to trying out new ways of relating to him. The development and use of such insight is dependent upon the client's goals, including new goals presumably induced by new insight. Thus, examination of the client's behavior and perceptions must be continuously referenced to his task: what can he learn about himself, others, or his circumstances that will better enable him to achieve what he wants to achieve.

Helping the client increase his awareness is an effort in individualized education. For optimal teaching and learning in the interview, we assume that the client and caseworker must have mutual respect and that each must trust the other is well-intentioned. But more than this, the client, like any learner, must be able to comprehend what he is being taught and see its relation to larger wholes. If the practitioner's communication is responsive, his formulations should fit into the client's way of looking at things, and so they should be understandable to him. At the same time, they should add in each case increments to the edge of his awareness. In addition, the client needs to appreciate the intent and directions of the caseworker's formulations. The caseworker points out to a father his pattern of promising to do things with his son and then backing down. The father needs to see that the understanding of such a pattern is a prerequisite to changing it and that a change in his response may lead to desired improvement in his relationship with his son—if that is the goal. It is sometimes erroneously assumed that a client does not need to comprehend what the caseworker is up to when he uses insight-oriented techniques, or that the client will somehow "catch on" as treatment proceeds.

The concentration of the caseworker's awareness-enhancing efforts upon specific aspects of the client's functioning and situation should facilitate the client's learning. Particular actions or events can be examined in the depth of detail that is sometimes necessary to bring about changes in perceptions. The client is less able to drift to other areas of discussion as a defense against sometimes painful, but helpful, self-disclosure. The degree of focus called for in the model should enable the caseworker to specify with some precision the cognitive changes he is attempting to achieve. He then should be able to determine if there is any evidence that these changes are occurring and are being put to use. The resulting feedback can then be used to guide his subsequent efforts. For example, a husband might perceive his wife in a distorted and over-simplified way as being "totally inconsistent" in her handling of the children. The caseworker may decide that some correction in this perception is necessary to enable the husband and wife to achieve a shared task of being mutually supportive in their handling of the children. He attempts to help the husband see his wife more realistically by calling his attention to various consistencies that do exist in his wife's behavior toward the children. The practitioner should then watch for and, if necessary, elicit evidence as to whether his client is, in fact, seeing his wife differently and, if so, whether the altered perception is having any apparent effect on his behavior. If the desired effects are not being achieved, then steps can be taken. More intensive efforts to correct the perception can be continued directly with the client, or a shift to alternative methods of effecting change in his behavior may be seen as the best course to follow.

It is unrealistic to expect the caseworker to go through this process with every cognitive change he is attempting to effect but he should with those he deems of major importance. If we are basing much of our treatment strategy on our ability to alter behavior through enhancing the client's awareness, then a close checking of the results of our efforts seems called for.

New understanding may not in itself be sufficient to bring about alterations in behavior. Other techniques need to be brought to bear to help the client translate insight into action. Operations which will subsequently be described—encouragement, direction, and interventions in the client's social network—play important functions in augmenting forces for change set in motion by increased awareness. Thus, a client may have been helped to understand that he has trouble getting to work on time because of an exaggerated need to assert his independence against authority, and he may be helped to appreciate the consequences of his late arrivals; but encouragement, practical advice, and the help of his spouse may also be needed to bring about the desired change in behavior.

Practitioners using this model should make use of the very sizable literature in which different insight oriented methods are presented and illustrated. Three sources are particularly relevant: 1) models of short-term psychotherapy which rely heavily on such methods (e.g., Malan, 1963; McGuire, 1965a, 1965b; Wolberg, 1965; Sifneos, 1967); 2) descriptions of use of techniques of this kind within the context of short-term casework (e.g., Gilbert, 1960; Murray and Smitson, 1963; Parad, 1963; Epstein, 1965; Oppenheimer, 1967; Reid and Shyne, 1969; Kerns, 1970; Rapoport, 1970; Small, 1971; 3) the work of Florence Hollis (1964, 1967a, 1967b, 1968), who has carefully and lucidly detailed the variety of specific procedures caseworkers use to enhance the client's understanding. Although these procedures are cast in a rather different casework model, they can readily be adapted to the requirements of brief, time-limited treatment.

ENCOURAGEMENT. A caseworker makes use of encouragement when he expresses approval or some other kind of positive reaction to actions the client has undertaken, is carrying out, or is contemplating. The term also applies to endorsements of the client's attitudes which might be expected to give rise to certain actions. In using encouragement, the caseworker does not present formulations which add substantially to the client's awareness; rather he *responds* to actions the client has carried out or is contemplating, or to characteristics he may possess. Simple direct expressions of approval —"good" or some equivalent term, or even a smile or nod of the head—are the most common forms of this type of communication. But encouragement can also be conveyed in more elaborate or less direct ways: "It looks like you have made a start by contacting the employment agency"; "You know you have the ability to get passing grades"; "I am impressed that you were able to keep control of your temper!"

In the present model, encouragement is used primarily to strengthen and stimulate behavior that might be expected to contribute to progress toward the tasks. It is thus used selectively rather than as a routine response to whatever the caseworker might find commendable in the client or his actions.

The caseworker must then keep in mind what actions are to be encouraged and how. It is assumed that the caseworker's approval of actions the client has already taken will have the effect of encouraging further actions of the same type. Thus, if the caseworker commends a mother for her firmness with her child in a particular situation, he is in effect encouraging her to display a similar kind of firmness in similar situations.

In theory, encouragement contributes to change since the client is likely to favor actions that will result in the approval and endorsement of a person he presumably respects. The positive response of the caseworker is assumed to be a source of some gratification for the client and, hence, should tend to reinforce his behavior. Cast in these terms, encouragement may be viewed as one form of positive reinforcement, as the term is used in theories of learning. Hence, such theories, as well as their empirical bases and practical applications, are relevant.

There is ample evidence (reviewed by Krasner, 1971) to demonstrate that positive reinforcement provided by practitioners in the form of approval, encouragement, and the like can alter problematic behavior of clients and patients. It is not clear, however, how positive reinforcement in this form is most effectively used in respect to the complex behavior dealt with in casework situations. To what classes of behavior does it apply? Under what conditions does the caseworker's encouragement constitute reinforcement and what determines its strength? Questions of this kind are being addressed in the work of practitioners attempting to utilize principles of operant conditioning in casework (Stuart, 1967; Thomas, 1970; Gambrill, Thomas, and Carter, 1971). The results of this work should contribute to the theory and use of encouragement in the present system of treatment.

DIRECTION.* Responses in this category convey to the client the caseworker's advice or recommendations about possible sources of action the client might take as a part of his work on the task. In contrast to encouragement in which the caseworker endorses actions the client has initiated, direction proposes action possibilities the client has not considered or at

---

* Certain portions of this section have been adapted from William J. Reid and Barbara L. Shapiro, "Client Reactions to Advice," *Social Service Review*, June 1969, pp. 165–73.

least puts the caseworker on record as recommending one of several courses the client may be considering.

The caseworker's suggestion may be stated emphatically ("I think that you should join the club") or tentatively ("Perhaps you could try asking for a transfer") or implicitly ("Have you considered calling this to his attention?").

Giving the client direct advice about his problems has been viewed by casework theorists as a technique of limited and dubious value. Although one finds efforts to specify circumstances in which advice-giving may be profitably used, one is more impressed with the cautions against its possible overuse. Thus, "not criticizing or advising" were among Hamilton's (1951) desiderata of a positive casework response to a client. More recently, Hollis (1964) stated that "only the beginner or the clumsy worker makes major use of advice."

There is evidence to indicate that professional caseworkers are, in fact, quite chary in their use of advice. Studies based on content analysis of written and electronic recordings of casework interviews have reported fairly low percentages of caseworker communication classified as advice or its equivalent—from 1.5 to 5.2 percent in one group of studies reviewed by Mullen (1968). Moreover, in tests of casework practice under simulated conditions, advice-giving tends to be one of the least preferred ways of responding to the client.

On the other hand, there is evidence to suggest that people seeking help for psychological and interpersonal problems expect, and want, advice in larger quantities than they are likely to receive. In their study of expectations of psychotherapy, Garfield and Wolpin (1963) comment that, "although a majority of the respondents believe that an understanding of one's self is important in psychotherapy, they still prefer advice and expect that a moderate amount of therapy time will be devoted to such an activity." Similarly Heine and Trosman (1960) found that patients predominantly subscribed to a "guidance-cooperation" model of treatment while the therapists favored a "mutual participation" model. In their report of a study which examined the reactions of 183 clients to casework service, Reid and Shapiro (1969) reported that "lack of advice giving by the caseworker" was the client's most frequent complaint about service. If the caseworker was relatively high on his use of advice (5 to 10 percent of his responses), clients were less likely to be dissatisfied than if the caseworker made little use of this technique (less than 3 percent of his responses). Interestingly enough, only two clients in the entire sample complained that caseworkers gave "too much advice."

As several studies have indicated, the gap between the amount of advice expected and the amount delivered may be especially large for lower-class clients and patients. In fact, Hollingshead and Redlich (1952) go so far as to state that *the most frequent* source of difficulty between the lower status patient in psychotherapy and the therapist is the patient's tacit or overt demand for an authoritarian attitude on the part of the psychotherapist and the psychiatrist's unwillingness to assume this role, since it runs counter to certain therapeutic principles" (p. 345; italics added). If such findings apply to casework, then caseworkers who give little advice may fail to meet certain expectations of their clients. While available evidence suggests that clients would be more satisfied with service if caseworkers increased their level of advice-giving (beyond the 5 or so percent level that seems to be the current norm) we still have little evidence on the effectiveness of this particular technique in bringing about change. Moreover, in most studies direction or advice-giving is classified without reference to what the advice is about. Although we continue the same practice, it is with recognition that this category encompasses interventions of widely divergent qualities, from a passing suggestion about how to get Johnny to eat his vegetables to a recommendation that a family member be institutionalized.

In the present model, the worker's direction is of course bounded by the nature of the task. With this constraint, a practitioner cannot offer advice indiscriminately or gratuitously, a possible temptation with a suggestible or dependent client. Once the task has been set, direction, like other techniques, is concentrated on the means of helping the client achieve his goal; hence the caseworker is not put into the position of feeling obligated to advise the client on some major decision falling outside the structure of the task, even if the client requests it.

There is evidence (Reid, 1967) that direction is used to a greater extent in brief than in extended casework and we would expect that this technique would receive relatively heavy use in the present model. It serves two functions: 1) to give the client specific recommendations that, if carried out, may further his task accomplishment; 2) to provide him with an important source of cognitive and emotional stimulation —as a prod to constructive thought and action.

Clients frequently try out what caseworkers suggest to good advantage. But we are all familiar with the paradox of the client who seeks advice but never seems to use it. We have tended to assume that our recommendations are of little avail if the client does not carry them out, one reason, perhaps, why many practitioners make so little use of this technique.

The second function we attribute to direction may help explain this paradox. That the client fails to follow through on the worker's suggestion may not really matter. What the suggestion triggers off in the mind and feelings of the client may be the crucial consideration. For example, a suggestion may point up the lack of constructive behavior in a certain area, thereby causing the client to consider why this lack exists. Or a client may reject a piece of advice as unrealistic, but at the same time be stimulated to think of other courses of action he could take. Or, more generally, a recommendation from the caseworker may be part of a challenging, confronting approach that may open up productive areas of communication with the client.

It may be true that these functions could be achieved through other means, but it may also be true that the typical client desires this kind of give-and-take and finds it profitable. This interpretation may explain why clients are disappointed when a certain amount of advice is not forthcoming, even though they might not have acted upon whatever advice was actually given. Although the quality of the advice is obviously important, the crucial aspect of quality may be found, not in the soundness of the course of action recommended, but rather in what the recommendation may evoke.

Support for this view may be found in a study by Davis (1971). Davis obtained two kinds of data on the reactions of a group of seventeen mothers to caseworkers' advice about the problems of their children: one kind consisted of parents' immediate reactions to workers' advice in the treatment interviews (which were tape recorded and analyzed); the other, of parents' assessments elicited in a follow-up research interview. She found that a parent's reactions to a caseworker's direction in the treatment interview tended to be more negative than positive. Yet none thought the caseworker used too much advice; about a third wanted the caseworker to make greater use of this technique; and all but three could remember a piece of helpful advice. Few could recall any advice that was not helpful. One interpretation for these anomalous findings is that the mothers were receiving some useful stimulation from advice that they might have found "off the mark" at the time it was given. This interpretation is supported by the finding that all the mothers but two reported that the caseworker's suggestions called attention to their need to work on particular problems.

The only limit posed by the present model on the use of direction is that it be aimed at furthering the client's progress on the task. Thus the practitioner may base his suggestions on whatever theories of behavior he sees fit. In work with parents around problems of children, caseworkers have tended to base their suggestions on psychoanalytic theories of child development, but there are many other possibilities. In one case (Mrs. P), a practitioner, used direction based upon operant theory to enable a mother to carry out her task of helping her two boys overcome bedwetting. Following the caseworker's suggestions the mother set up a reward system in which small sums of money and other privileges were to be given the boys for dry nights or for changing sheets on wet beds. The mother was also directed to record relevant behavior (hers and the children's) related to this task so that it was possible to accumulate data which could be used as a basis for suggesting modification in the regime. The boys' bedwetting, which had been a chronic problem, was brought under control. From our point of view the practitioner made use of direction to help a mother with a task relating to her role performance, although from another point of view the practitioner used principles of operant conditioning to modify the boys' bedwetting. One might also regard the case as illustrating a "mixed-model" approach. We prefer to see it as exemplifying the range of intervention possibilities that is possible within the framework of the present model.

CHAPTER EIGHT

THE CONTEXT OF COMMUNICATION

In the present model, as in casework generally, the practitioner's communication is shaped by the context in which it occurs. An interview with a client provides one sort of context; a conference with a teacher about a youngster in treatment supplies another. In this chapter we will consider the practitioner's communication in its two principal contexts: the interview with the client and interchanges with individuals other than the client.

THE STRUCTURE OF THE INTERVIEW

The structure of initial interviews with clients flows from the preliminary steps of the model; that is, one begins with problem exploration and proceeds to task formulation and determination of durational limits. The structure of interviews devoted to work on the task is more complex and fluid but some general guidelines can be set forth.

Interviews concerned with work on the task generally begin with a review of what has been attempted and accomplished since the preceding visit. Whatever the caseworker or the client had agreed to do, is taken up. Thus, the caseworker may report on progress he has made in securing certain services for the client; the client may recount his efforts to be more considerate of his wife. Normally, the focus is on the client's activity, but always in relation to the task. The caseworker's opening question could be: "Have you been able to make any more progress in getting your mother to take care of herself?" It should never be the stock in trade. "How have things been going this past week?" The caseworker may then explore what the client has attempted, what has been achieved, what obstacles have been encountered, and so on. In addition to exploration the caseworker makes use of encouragement to reinforce actions that are moving the client toward task achievement.

From this point, the interview might go in any one of several directions, depending on what emerged during the initial review. Priority should be given to issues concerning the validity and nature of the task. In his recounting of what he has done, the client may raise, directly or indirectly, questions about the validity of the task itself. He may minimize its importance, shift to other topics and the like. His concerns about the worthwhileness of the task, in whatever form they are expressed, should be taken up before proceeding further with the interview. If he ignores or leaves the task to talk of other problems, an effort should be made to defer consideration of them until his position vis-à-vis the task has been dealt with. More often, questions will arise concerning the nature of the task. Thus, the initial review of progress may lead to attempts to further clarify or specify the task or to delineate sub-tasks. A couple may have reported some progress in their efforts to be more supportive of one another in the disciplining of their children, but one or both may have questions about how much mutual support is necessary or desirable. An elderly man who is trying to locate a permanent living arrangment may have decided not to pursue a previous plan to investigate a home for the aging and wonders what he should do next. In such instances, the caseworker and client must attempt to consider more specifically what the task is or what further steps it might require.

Once questions about the nature or validity of the task have been dealt with—or if no questions of this sort arise—the caseworker's efforts are directed at helping the client carry forward his work on the task. Communication between the caseworker and client is largely concerned with why the client is unable to carry out actions or with how the client can best effect them.

Exploration and structuring are used to elicit or focus communications from the client. From this informational base, the caseworker develops and presents formulations about the client's behavior, his interactions, and situation; he makes suggestions, provides encouragement, or explains actions he could take on the client's behalf outside the interview. These techniques are used in whatever combinations seem best calculated to help the client progress with the task. Until more is known about the effect of different methods under different conditions, trial-and-error with the individual client is perhaps the most sensible approach. Certainly no premium is placed on any one method, that is, enhancing the client's awareness is not assumed to have any more intrinsic merit than direction.

If concurrent tasks are being worked on, the format is repeated for each task. If the tasks are closely related, or can be linked through some common denominator in the client's behavior or situation, then the caseworker may move the discussion back and forth between tasks or take up themes cutting across tasks.

The final portion of the interview is devoted to consideration of what the client and caseworker are to work on prior to their next meeting. When treatment is brief, it is important to make maximum use of intervals between interviews.

In the present model, one of the more important functions of the interview is, in fact, to provide a medium for planning activities outside its limits. For the client, these activities may range from taking specific steps (such as contacting an employment agency) to attempting to try out new ways of responding to situations (such as sticking to a schedule of time to be spent in academic work). As might be expected, considerable use is made of direction and encouragement in working out such assignments with the client.

Caseworkers have always attached much importance to what the client does after he leaves the session. In fact, we even have a cliché for it: "Most treatment takes place outside the interview." But usually, what the client is to work on between interviews is left rather vague ("Think about this some more") and in normal practice is not even discussed with the client.

Clients do try out things discussed in interviews without the benefit of special planning, and the thrust of casework, whatever form it takes, is to affect the client's "real life" behavior. But planning specifically with the client how he can work on his problem between interviews offers a useful way of both structuring and stimulating his problem-solving efforts.

AN ILLUSTRATIVE INTERVIEW

The example to follow illustrates some of the generalizations we made about interviews concerned with work on the task, and also provides additional examples of the techniques and strategies of the model. The interview is drawn from the middle phase of treatment with a woman, Mrs. Yost, who was trying to "make the best of a poor marriage" for the "sake of the children." Since her husband refused to be seen by the caseworker, it was decided to work with Mrs. Yost alone. Of her many complaints about the marriage, there seemed to be two she could do something about: her husband's unwillingness to participate in any kind of social activities with her, and his "stinginess" in money matters. Three concurrent tasks were formulated for her to work on: 1) to try to get him to do more with her socially; 2) to develop more of a social life of her own; 3) to work out a more satisfactory financial arrangement with her husband.

The interview (the fifth) opened with the client's recounting of her effort the previous weekend to get her husband to go with her and another couple to the beach. (She and the caseworker had agreed during the previous interview that she should make this attempt since she knew the wife of this couple was going to ask them to go.) Her husband, after first promising to go along, backed off at the last minute so that Mrs. Yost had to go with them by herself. The caseworker explored the episode with her to determine if she had behaved in a way that might have caused Mr. Yost not to follow through but could find no evidence that she had. Mrs. Yost then proceeded to put this episode together with several others in a general complaint that it was useless "to try to get her husband out of the house." The client's questioning of the validity of the task was taken up, leading to a review of her previous efforts to involve her husband in similar outings or even to get him to go out by themselves. There had been far more failures than successes. She was ready to give up. In this discussion, the caseworker presented certain formulations designed to give her a more balanced, differentiated view of her husband: now and then, at least, he did take her places, although usually with some reluctance. Mrs. Yost felt, however, that "it really wasn't worth the effort." The caseworker (with some misgivings) agreed that perhaps more headway could be made in other areas. (From this point on this task was given only minor emphasis and little progress was achieved.)

The caseworker returned to the episode Mrs. Yost had related earlier in the interview, drawing attention to the fact that she had gone alone with the couple. Through this means discussion was shifted to the second task, increasing the scope of her own life outside the home. This task, which had originally been seen as a way of supplementing the hoped for results of the first task, had now perhaps become an alternative route to her need for social activities. Her decision to go with the friends was commented on positively by the caseworker. Consideration was then given to whether or not she should go by herself to a cook-out to which these same friends had invited her and her husband. She revealed her reluctance to go places like this by herself, although she acknowledged that she usually had a good time. Her uneasiness about "going it alone" was taken up as an obstacle to this particular task. Her feeling that "it didn't look right" to go places without her husband seemed to play a part, a feeling complicated by her resentment at her husband for putting her in such situations. While recognizing that anyone might feel that way, the case-worker made the point that she seemed to be reacting pretty strongly to what others might think of her. Her wish to do more on her own was reconsidered and reaffirmed as a better alternative than "doing nothing." The caseworker encouraged her determination to "do something" and suggested she go by herself to the cook-out if her husband were unwilling to go along.

Mrs. Yost herself switched the focus to the remaining task. In the prior interview, the task had been specified as one of her trying to get her husband to give her a lump sum of money each week, rather than giving her only as much as was necessary for the purpose at hand. Her having to ask for small amounts to buy special items was a constant source of humili-ation for her and of bickering between them. In ensuing dis-cussions of how she might go about this, Mrs. Yost expressed (as she had in the previous interview) her fears of asking her husband for money, particularly if she thought a quarrel would result. She indicated that she had "a thing" about money, revealing that her father used to give her small sums unexpectedly which she would take as a sign of his affection. The caseworker did not pursue this lead however; rather he asked Mrs. Yost if she thought she could ask her husband for the money. Despite her fears, she was willing to give it a try and they worked out a plan for discussing this with him, which included presenting him with a list of her regular ex-penses.

Caseworker: What if he refuses?
Mrs. Yost: (thoughtful, then abruptly) I think I would leave him.

Caseworker: Would you tell him this?

Mrs. Yost: Yes.

Caseworker: Good.

It was agreed that Mrs. Yost would present her plan to her husband the first thing the following week.

As can be seen, this interview follows the general paradigm set forth earlier. Although it covered more tasks than is usual, or perhaps desirable, the caseworker's task-centered orientation comes through quite clearly. His techniques were concentrated on furthering task achievement rather than on helping the client express feeling or develop insight *per se*. His decision not to pick up on the client's tantalizing references to her father exemplifies this orientation. Given the client's momentum at this point, it did not seem necessary to discuss this historical material in order to further her progress on the task. Had she been unable to act on the task, then the caseworker might well have decided that possible psychodynamic connections between her father, husband, and money should be examined.

The outcome of this case as a whole was moderately successful. Although Mrs. Yost was unable to get her husband more involved in social activities, she did begin to get out more with friends on her own. Her husband, rather to her surprise, "gave in" without much opposition to her request that she be given a lump sum of money on a regular basis. She ended treatment quite satisfied with her progress, particularly in respect to the money, and she thought her marriage had become a lot more tolerable. Some day, she said, she would leave her husband if things did not get better, but now was not the time.

COMMUNICATION IN MULTIPLE INTERVIEWS

The term "multiple interview" is used to designate an interview involving the caseworker and two or more clients. Most multiple interviews in casework take place with family members: a husband and wife; a parent and child; or entire families. In task-centered casework, multiple interviews are used most extensively for problems of interpersonal conflict but may be used in relation to any problem involving more than one client. Thus far our efforts to conceptualize the caseworker's communications have been restricted to individual interviews. We have not yet worked out a technology for multiple interviews. Systematic attempts to classify the caseworker's activities in multiple interviews have consisted largely of extensions of taxonomies developed for individual interviews (Abrams et al., 1966; Ehrencranz, 1967a, 1967b; Hollis, 1968). These studies have demonstrated that basic modes of caseworker communication used in individual interviews can be applied to multiple interviews but also have indicated that not all operations can be properly accounted for through schemes designed for one-to-one relationships.

It certainly makes sense to try to develop one comprehensive system for classifying the caseworker's activities rather than separate systems for individual as opposed to multiple interviews. We see no reason why the five basic categories of communication we have presented above cannot be adapted to multiple interviews. Thus, in task-centered treatment carried on through family interviews, the practitioner would use exploration with family members to elicit and clarify target problems, would attempt to structure their communication in relation to the task, might help them gain greater awareness of their patterns of interaction, and would probably provide encouragement and direction to individual members or to the family as a whole. In addition, it would be necessary to keep track of the intended receivers of the practitioner's messages and to develop ways of accounting for his functions as facilitator and analyst of communication among family members that takes place in the interview. Moreover, an operation used in individual interviews may assume quite different forms when applied to family interviews. It is one thing to help the individual client focus his talk on the task; it is quite another thing to set up a sub-task for family members to work on in the interview; yet both operations would fall in the structuring category.

The basic strategy of the model applies to whatever form the interview takes, and the interview form flows from the nature of the target problems, tasks and durational limits. We have little to say at this point about how various techniques may be applied in multiple interviews. The best we can do is to point the practitioner in the general direction of literature on the subject with the hope that he can make appropriate applications to our model. He may find the following works of particular interest: Sherman (1959); Geist and Gerber (1960); Jackson and Weakland (1961); Satir (1964); Carroll (1968); Haley and Hoffman (1967); and Scherz (1970).

We have already presented several case examples that provide some illustrations of the use of multiple interviews in the present model. The following example will illustrate more fully the application of this technique.

Dora Alton, fifteen, was referred by her physician because she had taken an overdose of pills. Her mother brought her at once for medical care so there was no physical aftermath of this suicidal gesture. Dora was brought to the agency by her mother but she was seen alone first. The mother had, in a sense, handed her over to the social worker to be in some way taken care of. Although Dora readily described how she had gone into the medicine closet and sampled two of each type of pill she found there, she was laconic otherwise and did not elaborate on how she was feeling or what was upsetting her. Pressed to reveal what she thought her problem was, she did say that her mother was too strict, but she could not elaborate. The mother was then seen alone. She disclaimed knowledge or understanding about why Dora would have attempted suicide. This was a black, fatherless family, welfare recipients, with three children: a son, nineteen, who was employed and gave most of his earnings to support the household; Ellen, a seventeen-year-old in high school; and Dora. Mrs. Alton was an intelligent and capable woman who managed better than most on her meager income. Both girls were doing well in school and seemed to have friends. Mother said spontaneously, as if turning it over in her mind, that her own sister had told her that she is too strict with her children. There were implied questions put to the social worker. Was she too strict? Did her strictness have anything to do with Dora's upset?

Since both mother and daughter were apparently perceiving the problem as conflict over "strictness," it was suggested that they both be seen together. It was then discovered that Ellen had come along and was in the waiting room. All three were interviewed immediately as a family group. There was no real problem in communication with the social worker when the three converged. Mother was the most talkative, Ellen second, and Dora least, but all three took an active part. Within a matter of minutes, it was clear that the mother's strictness was the burning issue for all three. Strictness meant that the mother laid down detailed rules of behavior to govern her daughters' relations with boys and then she grilled the girls after social encounters to check on obedience. The older brother joined his mother in this program. Agreement emerged in this interview that the family's task would be to devise rules of social conduct which would be more acceptable to the girls and would still fulfill the mother's obligation to protect them. Eight family sessions were planned. During the course of treatment, exploration was used to secure data on the interaction between the mother and her daughters and structuring was used to focus discussion on those interactions relating to the task. The caseworker helped the three to gain a better understanding of each other's motives and expectations concerning the "strictness" issue. Encouragement and direction were employed to bring about modifications in the mother's rules for social conduct and the daughters' behavior in respect to them.

As often happens, treatment appeared to falter in the middle phase. The mother found excuses and came only every other time. She was having the worst of it because she was the one who had to give up something, but she agreed to continue to participate. The girls began practicing ways to make their needs and views known at home instead of going alone into the bedroom where they railed at brother and mother secretly. With the caseworker's help, the clients developed the rule that when mother interfered she had to explain and justify herself and the daughters had to respond verbally and negotiate with her.

COMMUNICATIONS WITH COLLATERALS

Hollis (1964) observed that most of the casework procedures she had identified in her studies of direct treatment of clients paralleled the kinds of professional activities carried out by caseworkers with those other than the client. As Hollis notes (p. 76), one of the present authors (Reid) had suggested this idea to her.

At first glance it may seem strange to think of the caseworker's efforts in the client's environment as being of the same order as his operations with the client. We are used to viewing them in quite different terms. The idea begins to make sense, however, when we realize that the environment the caseworker works with consists largely of individuals, including relatives, physicians, teachers, nurses, foster parents, lawyers, police, housing officials, psychologists, and social workers. The caseworker's efforts to affect the client's environment consists largely of communicating with such persons, whom we call collaterals.

We can see that the caseworker's communications have certain common characteristics whether they are addressed to the client or some one else. With others, as well as with the client, he is receiving and giving information to accomplish certain goals. This view enables us to specify a set of common, observable referents for the caseworker's activities wherever they occur and permits us to place these activities within a single conceptional framework. It also helps bridge the dichotomy between work with clients and "non-clients," one that becomes particularly troublesome in cases in which individuals, such as foster parents and relatives, fall somewhere between our customary distinctions of who is a client and who is not. We shall now attempt to spell out these ideas in more detail by considering how certain techniques used in communication with the clients are employed in communications with collaterals.

Just as exploration is the most frequently used type of communication with clients it is also probably the most common operation used with others. In large part it serves as an extension of the data-seeking the caseworker engages in with the client. It may begin with a review of earlier recording, if the client is previously known to the agency, or the taking in of whatever "referral information," both written and oral, the caseworker may be given prior to his first meeting with the client. The data may be in written form and the caseworker may read rather than listen, but he is still obviously engaging in a form of communication with others who have information to transmit about the client. After his initial interview and between subsequent interviews the caseworker may continue to use exploration to increase his fund of information about the client; records may be secured and individuals with special knowledge of the client may be consulted, all of course with the client's consent. In addition exploration is used as the basis for bringing about change in a manner analogous to its use in communication with the client. If the target problem is inadequate resources, the caseworker may explore what various organizations may have to offer his client with the intent of locating the necessary resources. As in the process of getting information about the client, the caseworker may lay the groundwork for perceptual, attitudinal and behavioral changes on the part of others toward the client. For example, detailed exploration of a teacher's knowledge about a child's classroom behavior may provide the basis for changes in her point of view about the child.

While structuring and encouragement as used with the client have their parallels in communications with collaterals, we would like to devote our attention to the more frequently used techniques of enhancing awareness and direction.

Enhancing awareness is used principally with collaterals to help them arrive at a better understanding of the client and his circumstances. In providing this understanding, the caseworker's usual intent is to shape the actions of others toward the client or to initiate action. Thus the caseworker may help a physician see why a particular patient is resisting surgery, may try to give a judge an appreciation of factors contributing to an adolescent's delinquency, or give information on a family's needs to a resource-providing agency. While efforts to help collaterals develop awareness of their own behavior are not used extensively, still such techniques may be employed with relatives, foster parents, and others who assume quasi-client roles, or with other professionals, such as teachers, in "intensive" consultative relationships. When used they are directed to kinds of self-understanding germane to the individual's behavior toward the client.

Direction is used principally to recommend actions that might benefit the client. A cottage parent might be advised to be firmer with an impulse-ridden child; a homemaker might be given detailed instructions about caring for a handicapped person; or a staff member of another agency might be asked that the agency provide a certain service for a client. The caseworker's advice may reflect expert opinion, as in the first example above, may be backed by formal authority, as in the second, or may be an expression of advocacy in the client's behalf, as in the final example.

The qualities of practitioner communication characterizing face-to-face interchange with clients also apply to interchanges with collaterals. It is particularly important that communications are systematic. If the caseworker designs his efforts at helping the client carry out the task, then his activities with others should be task-relevant. If so, they must of necessity be related to the caseworker's communications with the client. Thus in one case, that of Mr. D, the client's task was to secure home-bound employment. Through exploration with the client the caseworker obtained a picture of the client's interests and capacities; through exploration of resources he was able to locate an agency that could provide the client with the kind of employment the client wanted. In the process the caseworker helped the client to understand the agency's requirements and enabled agency staff to get a picture of the client's special needs and limitations.

CHAPTER NINE

TERMINATION

IN TASK-CENTERED casework, the process of termination begins in the initial phase as the client and worker agree upon the time span and on the number and spacing of interviews for the whole sequence of treatment. As work proceeds the practitioner makes periodic references to the number of interviews and the amount of time remaining.

In the next-to-last or final interview, attention should shift to helping the client identify achievements and plan further task work he may carry out on his own. In most cases, tasks are not fully achieved at point of closing. In many closed tasks the client may need to carry out additional steps; open tasks, by definition, can never be fully completed. Discussion is usually centered on the client's future activities in relation to his tasks or to other aspects of the problems that have been worked on. In cases involving concurrent tasks, the task given secondary attention during the course of treatment may be emphasized, particularly if little remains to be done on the primary task. What the client may be able to do about problems not dealt with in treatment may be considered, although at this time the practitioner should avoid bringing up difficulties the client is reluctant to discuss. Talk of the client's further problem-solving efforts should not override the importance given to what the client has accomplished. In the planned short-term cases surveyed by Parad and Parad (1968b), it was found that the typical client responded to termination with "positive feelings of mastery or achievement" (p. 419). It is this kind of reaction that the caseworker should attempt to bring about and preserve.

The client or the practitioner, or both, may be reluctant to terminate treatment at the agreed-upon stopping point. The client may feel pangs of loss at the prospect of breaking off a meaningful relationship or may think that he has not accomplished enough or not enough has been done for him. The caseworker may be more impressed by problems remaining than by what has been accomplished.

As Aldrich (1968) has said, "the prestige and tradition of thoroughness of psychoanalysis and its derivatives—'long-term' psychotherapy or intensive casework tend to reinforce the therapist's option to continue treatment rather than to live with the uncertainty of letting the patient or client take over before all goals are completely attained" (p. 113). Sometimes, the caseworker and client may interact in ways to produce an apparent common desire to prolong treatment, even though neither party had this in mind. The client may be ready to end treatment, although he may have misgivings about this step. The caseworker may have decided that little more can be accomplished, although he feels guilty about "short-changing" the client. Such feelings may prove to be mutually reinforcing with the result that the relationship may be continued even though its essential purpose has been served.

In our judgment, most "termination problems" of this kind do not arise if a clear and firm agreement on the limits of service is reached by the practitioner and client at the beginning and used as a reference point during the course of treatment. If so, the client is less likely to build up an expectation of an indefinite relationship and the caseworker is compelled to tailor his therapeutic ambitions to the limits that have been set. If the caseworker accepts the theories about the nature of problem-change and the mobilizing effect of time limits advanced in this book, he should be able to set and stick to these limits with conviction. If he does not, then he should probably not be using the model.

The organizational context is also important. Practitioners will feel more comfortable about terminating on time if short-term treatment is the basic service offered or if short-term work has the sanction and support of the agency's administrators and supervisors. Through our own clinical experience and consultations with caseworkers in various settings we have become acutely aware of how difficult it is for a practitioner to present a completed eight-interview case to a supervisor who is convinced that it takes that long just to establish a relationship with the client.

As noted previously, only a small proportion of clients who complete courses of planned brief service express a desire for extended treatment. Extensions of the original treatment contract—usually no more than a few sessions—normally suffice for most clients. Such extensions are indicated when further work may help the client make significant additional progress on the task or when the client's reequilibration is upset by critical events at the point of termination.

We see nothing inconsistent in offering long-term treatment to those clients who expressly request it during the course of task-centered casework or at its termination. Presumably these clients would be the self-selected few who might be expected to profit from it, although the caseworker might wish to help the client pin down what he hopes to achieve and to structure the projected course of extended treatment around explicit goals. The task focus we advocate can be used, of course, in long-term as well as short-term casework. We would encourage experimentation in that direction.

Issues arising around termination in planned short-term cases may present the practitioner with difficult dilemmas. Resolving uncertainties by routine extension of the contract runs the risk of pushing the client beyond the optimum limits of treatment, or at least of involving both him and the caseworker in unnecessary extra effort. Moreover, if predetermined end points of treatment are waived on the slightest pretext, the practitioners may cease to take them seriously with a resulting breakdown of the basic structure of the treatment design. On the other hand, holding hard and fast to the agreed upon termination date come what may, may deny needed help to certain clients. Although it cannot always be applied with certainty, the basic principle is that agreed-upon limits should be adhered to unless there are clear indications to the contrary.

For example, a flexible approach to termination seemed to make sense in the case of Mrs. B, an elderly, somewhat senile woman in need of eye surgery. She was referred to a medical social worker who agreed to work with her and her relatives to secure the necessary operation and to plan for her post-operative care. Due to uncontrollable vagaries in the hospital's scheduling of her surgery, the projected termination date for the task-centered sequence coincided with the date of her hospitalization. Although the initial task had been substantially completed—arrangements for post-operative care had already been worked out with her and her relatives—the caseworker decided that it would be wise to continue to see Mrs. B following the surgery and throughout the course of the short period of hospitalization which was to follow. Mrs. B had indicated she would appreciate visits from the caseworker after her surgery and there was general concern about the possible effect of surgery on her mental condition. The extension of service was based on Mrs. B's need to have someone she liked and trusted "look in on her"—the interviews were brief and informal—and a need to monitor her psychological reactions to surgery.

The use of a flexible approach to termination may have created more problems than it solved in the case of Mrs. N, who was referred to medical social service for problems concerning her eight-year-old son. His chronic and disabling illness required intensive home care which she was not providing properly; moreover she was ambivalent about permitting him to have corrective surgery which he needed in order to recover the use of his legs. In the course of ten interviews (the original contract) Mrs. N made excellent progress on her major task of providing adequate home care for her son; she also agreed to permit the corrective surgery.

The medical staff members were so delighted with Mrs. N's new-found cooperativeness and her improved care of the child that they began to exert subtle pressure on the practitioner to "hold on." If a little help can be so productive, hope soared for the prospects of a good deal more of the same. Not only that, but as termination approached, Mrs. N began to allude to problems she was experiencing with her other children and her boy friend. At the same time she also commented without any apparent sense of anxiety that the agreed-upon termination date was at hand.

That a client about to terminate a successful course of treatment should be ambivalent and give double messages about termination is not in the least surprising. When these messages were explored to find out if they meant a request for an extension in order to work on these problems, Mrs. N was noncommittal. The practitioner at this point proposed a five-session extension, which Mrs. N accepted. There was an anticlimatic aura to this extension. The practitioner was uncertain about how to proceed with the plethora of problems that Mrs. N appeared to have but seemed reluctant to pursue. Little further progress was made during this additional period.

Perhaps the caseworker needs to ask himself: "What specific purpose will be served by the extension?" "What precisely can we hope to accomplish in the additional period of time?" As the last case illustrates, one should not extend the period of service simply because the client has remaining problems or because the caseworker or others think the client "needs" more help (a judgment which in itself means nothing more than "our need to help this client has not yet been satisfied"). If the extension is substantial (consisting of more than two interviews) then perhaps the caseworker and client need to work out an explicit agreement on the focus of the additional work. It is best if the initiative for the extension comes from a client. If it comes from the caseworker, he should make his reasons clear to the client and make sure that the client sees potential value in the extension.

In some cases, the benefits from treatment will have been realized in advance of the termination date. The most clear-cut examples occur in closed tasks, which may be successfully completed early in a projected course of service. If the treatment contract involves only closed tasks which are completed ahead of schedule, then early termination is normally indicated. In fact, in cases of this kind, such an understanding should probably be part of the initial agreement between caseworker and client.

Open tasks present more complications in this respect. Initiative for early termination should normally come from the client rather than the caseworker. The caseworker then has to decide whether to try to "hold" the client to the original terms of the contract or accept his request for early termination. The first option is indicated if in his judgment the target problem has not been alleviated and if the client appears able to make further progress on the original tasks or seems capable of working successfully on other problem-reducing tasks that might be devised. If not, then the client's request should be accepted in a positive way—as a reflection of his successful mastery of the problem. In keeping with our basic position, considerable weight is given to the client's own perception of the status of his problem. If the client feels it has been substantially resolved and no further work is needed, then the caseworker should have good reasons, which he should make promptly clear to the client, why treatment should be continued to the terminal point originally agreed upon.

When an individual leaves a particular course of brief treatment he does not necessarily terminate his career as a client.

We do not see the client's returning for further help as an indicator of the insufficiency of an earlier treatment experience, even if he comes back for help with the same kind of problem. Problems of living are akin to certain kinds of physical conditions, like upper respiratory infections perhaps, which occur periodically and for which we may seek medical help from time to time if they became serious enough. If there were some "once and for all cure" for such conditions we would probably take it, but there is not. Similarly there is no definitive cure that we know of for problems of living.

By termination we hope that the client will have achieved a significant degree of relief from the one or two problems that he most wanted help with, at least enough relief so that he no longer wants further help *at that point*. We expect that he may want help again with other variations of the same problem or with some other kinds of problem and would encourage him to return if he does.

CHAPTER TEN

ADAPTATIONS OF THE MODEL

THERE IS no end to the special conditions or contingencies that need to be taken into account in the development of a general model of practice. Up to this point, our consideration of contingencies has been limited to those encountered in most practice situations—the client who does not acknowledge a problem, the client who presents a multiplicity of problems, and so on. In this chapter, we will take up a number of circumstances that arise in particular settings or fields of practice, and we will suggest ways in which our model may be adapted to these conditions, or vice-versa.

We had to be selective. We have tried to choose those contingencies which have a rather substantial impact upon a considerable portion of casework practice. In brief, we will consider how task-centered casework may be carried out in the following contexts: 1) in relation to programs of long-term care for children or other vulnerable groups in the population; 2) in interpersonal treatment of children; 3) in conjunction with provision of concrete services; 4) in treatment of acute, situational problems; 5) in the exercise of authoritative or protective functions.

LONG-TERM CARE RESPONSIBILITIES

Casework is practiced in many health and welfare organizations which have a responsibility for long-term care of such groups as children, the aged, the mentally retarded, the mentally ill, and individuals with chronic physical illness or disability. The task-centered model may offer an approach to casework treatment as a part of long-term care, without eschewing the social responsibilities such care entails.

The field of child welfare offers the most important examples of long-term helping commitments in social work. The cluster of agencies within this field provides a range of substitute care arrangements for children, such as foster homes and residential institutions. This sector of social work has been traditionally charged with the responsibility for overseeing the care, protection, and treatment of the children who enter its organizational network via the many routes to family breakdown. This responsibility has been viewed as extensive in scope and protracted in duration. Using this field of practice as an example, we will attempt to show how brief, task-centered casework, with some modifications, might be utilized in long-term care arrangements.

The caseworker's role in child welfare settings is likely to comprise a rather diverse mixture of responsibilities. Caseworkers normally carry out many "maintenance" functions which include providing supervision to foster parents; arranging for changes in foster homes; serving as a liaison between the natural parent, the child, and the agency; securing special resources for the child; and monitoring the child's mental and emotional development. These functions are designed primarily to maintain a certain system, which comprises the child and his caretakers, at an optimum level. While these functions are critical and may require a high degree of skill, they may be distinguished from treatment designed to alleviate complex psychosocial problems that may arise within this system. Usually, the caseworker is expected to deal with these problems as well.

When such psychosocial problems do arise, and if they fall within the scope of our model as most of them probably do, then our treatment approach could be applied. Tasks could be formulated as in the case of any target problem; the treatment sequence addressed to the problem at hand could be time-limited, even though the caseworker might continue his relationship with the child and his caretakers following termination of the sequence.

Within a long-term relationship then, there might be one or several segments of brief, task-centered treatment. The caseworker might take responsibility for identifying potential target problems and offering treatment. In keeping with the principles of this model, there would need to be explicit agreements on problems and tasks before treatment could proceed. Caseworkers would then be less likely to drift in and out of quasi-therapeutic relationships lacking clearly defined goals and structures.

The caseworker would be sensitive to possible target problems in the child's social network—his relations with foster and natural parents, school and peers, and the interactions between foster and natural parents. In particular, he might expect such problems to arise around "critical transitions" that occur in the careers of children who become agency responsibilities: the child's initial separation from his natural parents; his subsequent placement in a family or institution; changes from institutional to foster placement; changes in caretakers within a particular type of placement; and discharge from the child care system. Such transitions, with attendant ruptures in relationships and requirements to adapt to new situations, may generate the kinds of psychosocial problems that fall within the range of our model, although we would not foresee treatment *routinely* offered or given at such points.

If systematic intervention aimed at relief of specific target problems can be distinguished from other functions in child welfare practice, then much of what might be called interpersonal treatment can be brief and task-centered. This view would make possible different, and possibly more efficient, staffing patterns. For example, certain staff might become brief treatment specialists who could be called upon to intervene when potential target problems appeared; other staff could be given responsibility for long-term case management. If caseworkers with advanced training were used as the treatment specialist, one might avoid what Brieland (1968) has called the "unnecessary and indefensible . . . use [of] graduate social workers and other social workers interchangeably" (p. 5). If graduate caseworkers were not available for this role, then selected staff at the Bachelor's level (following some ideas advanced by Epstein, 1962) might be trained as specialists in brief treatment.

There might still be need for extended treatment relationships with certain children or natural parents. As in other settings, treatment of this sort could be reserved for special cases that would meet specified criteria. We hope that it would be guided by clearly stated goals and conducted within the structure of an explicitly designated therapeutic relationship, clearly distinguished from other functions.

The same considerations can be applied to other settings which provide extended care, such as facilities for the handicapped and chronically ill, homes for the aging, and mental hospitals. The needs for help expressed by clients in such settings are often around problems of living that can be treated through brief, task-centered casework. Short-term service can be given by the caseworker as a clearly defined segment of a long-term relationship which carries other functions used by the caseworker who serves as a treatment specialist. Sensitivity to potential target problems can be enhanced by use of the appropriate variations of the "critical transition" paradigm, which can be applied generally to any group that moves in, through, and out of extended care arrangements.

TREATMENT OF CHILDREN

Development of models for brief treatment of children has lagged behind work on short-term approaches for adults, even though a decade ago Eisenberg and Gruenberg (1961) concluded their review of research on the treatment of children with the observation that there was "lack of definite proof of the effectiveness of intensive psychotherapy" and that there had been a "tentative demonstration that short-term therapy produces equivalent symptomatic results" (p. 364). Use of brief treatment approaches with children seems to be gaining, however, as increasing numbers of clinicians appear to share

Nebl's view (1971) that short-term treatment of children's problems is a "versatile and effective method in selected cases" (p. 381). Recent studies of treatment services for children should certainly serve to stimulate further experimentation and model development. For example, the 1970 Report of the Joint Commission on Mental Health of Children identified at least nine prevalent modes of treatment for children, in addition to psychoanalysis and a large number of various psychotherapy approaches. Innovation and research to develop better methods of treatment were encouraged. The findings of the Commission are consistent with results of research on the effects of treatment with children (Levitt, 1963). Such studies provide no basis for confidence in existing approaches.

Thus, there is good reason to explore ways in which the present model may be adapted to direct treatment of children. Our efforts thus far, limited to a small number of clinical trials with adolescents and older children, suggest that the model can be applied without much difficulty to children, roughly age nine or older, who can participate effectively in treatment based largely on verbal communication. We have not yet explored possible modifications of the approach for very young children.

The high value placed on client autonomy seems to make the approach particularly intriguing and attractive to adolescents with whom it can be used in a fairly straightforward way. Certain adjustments, however, appear to be necessary with younger children who are less able to define problems and formulate tasks. Practitioners probably need to be more directive in helping the younger child through these steps, identifying possible problems the child is not able or is reluctant to verbalize, and formulating tasks which are appropriate to his age, family circumstances, and problem. Nevertheless, the working out of explicit agreements on the nature of the problem and the task should not be neglected.

Direct treatment of children is often combined with work with others in the child's environment, particularly family members and school personnel or, if the child is in placement, with foster parents and other caretakers. We favor this strategy whenever feasible. Because of his own immaturity and the powerful influences his environment can exert on his behavior, a child's efforts to carry out tasks need the active cooperation of others, often including complementary task work on the part of those responsible for his care. For this reason, among others, approaches in which parents and children work on shared or reciprocal tasks through the medium of family or multiple interviews, appear particularly promising.

No brief treatment model can provide solutions to all problems of children. Some behavioral disorders of children are the outgrowth of constitutional defects or psychopathological conditions, such as brain damage and autism. Disturbed behavior with such etiologies may not be responsive to the kind of brief treatment methods we advocate, although they may be useful in effecting modest changes in some cases. Certain family life styles may produce wholesale disruptions in normal processes of child development. Task-centered treatment is certainly not designed to change such life styles or to repair the resulting damage to the child's development. Other modalities are needed to pursue far-reaching goals of this kind.

The need for such treatment approaches, usually long-term and sometimes requiring institutionalization, cannot be questioned. But one can question the scope of their utility. In our view, "radical" long-term therapy aimed either at fundamental changes in family organization or the personalities of children has been used indiscriminately with far too many children who have failed to profit from it and perhaps did not need it in the first place.

The Joint Commission reported that 34 percent of children who were terminated from psychiatric clinic services in 1966 received a diagnosis of "transient situational personality disorder" (p. 268). It may be assumed that a significant proportion of children receiving other diagnoses were also exhibiting problems of limited duration. That such a large proportion of children brought to mental health facilities have transient or short-lived problems, suggests that short-term models, including the present one, might be used on a large scale in the treatment of children. If brief treatment fails, one can logically turn to more extensive therapy. It is difficult, if not illogical, to move in the opposite direction.

PROVISION OF CONCRETE SERVICE

In many settings tangible services, such as financial assistance, day care, and homemakers, are offered in conjunction with some form of casework. In fact, such services have been viewed as "components of casework," a view one is apt particularly to find in agencies in which casework is the major service modality. Even when the client is interested exclusively in the concrete service, it is often assumed that casework is necessary either as a means of enabling the client to make proper use of the concrete service or as a means of helping him with the "underlying" problem which may have given rise to the request for the service.

Although the tendency to mix the provision of concrete services with social treatment reflects a long-standing tradition in social work, there are developments which run counter to this practice. For example, where homemaker services are administered under the auspices of the medical and nursing professions, such services are not regarded as "components of casework," but as components of medical care. In European practice, homemaker service is likely to be provided as an independent entity. The current direction in the administration of public assistance is toward separation of income maintenance from other services, both tangible and intangible. These trends are in accord with our view that material assistance and counseling should be offered as separate services.

It is true that people in need of concrete services may also wish help for problems that are amenable to some form of interpersonal treatment, particularly if they perceive their problems as requiring some mixture of tangible assistance and counseling. Brief, task-centered casework could be the modality offered to the majority of such clients. The time span of treatment does not have to depend on the time span of a concrete service. In some cases, treatment might continue for a longer period; in others, the concrete service might go on after treatment has ended. For certain clients, of course, task-centered casework becomes a means of securing tangible resources. But this should be so only when the client needs the caseworker's intervention to obtain them.

If an agency offers a concrete service, then it should be available to clients who want it and who are able to meet what should be straightforward eligibility criteria. Clients can be informed of related counseling services without being expected to partake of them.

To use the provision of a tangible resource as a means of

building a "therapeutic" relationship with a client denies the client's right to decide for himself what kind of help he wants. To provide such a resource with the expectation that interpersonal help can somehow remove the need for it, is unrealistic, as had been shown in studies of unsuccessful efforts to use casework to "rehabilitate" families on public assistance: (Wallace, 1967; Mullen, Chazin, and Feldstein, 1970).

We see no need to adapt the present model to contingencies presented when the caseworker or his agency have material assistance to offer the client. Concrete services and casework can be seen as complementary but separate forms of help. Programs addressed to certain social problems may need both, but the kind of help given should flow, in our judgment, from the client's request rather than from the agencies' beliefs about what the client "really" needs.

How would this point of view work out in practice? Let us take as an example an agency with a program of "service to the aging." Its offerings include homemakers, temporary and supplementary financial assistance, friendly visiting by volunteers, a recreational center, and brief, task-centered casework. A client might request temporary financial assistance. If the client meets the agency's criteria for this kind of help, it would be given. Exploration of his life situation would be limited to information necessary to establish eligibility and the extent of financial need. If the client possessed problems that might be alleviated through casework he would be informed of the availability of this type of service and perhaps encouraged to try it, but there would be no expectation that he should. It would be up to him. Now, if the award of financial grants were made this simple, some would say, the agency's resources set aside for this purpose (probably meager to begin with) would soon be exhausted. A counter-argument would be this: if financial assistance is to be offered as a service (as is so advertised by many agencies) then sufficient resources should be allotted to make the service a genuine one within whatever limits are chosen. Casework should not be used (as it sometimes is) as a means of conserving the agency's financial resources. The same principles would apply to requests for other tangible services.

In some cases, clients would *request* help for problems that would fall within the scope of brief, task-centered casework. (Few problems in such a setting would require longer courses of casework.) Such requests might be made initially or might emerge in an application interview. For such clients, casework would be an appropriate service. As a part of this service, other resources of the agency might be utilized if they were relevant to the client's problem and task. An elderly client no longer able to care completely for himself might wish to talk to someone about finding a home for the aging. In the process of working on this problem of social transition, it might be decided that a combination of a "permanent" homemaker and a volunteer visitor would be the preferred plan, and the agency's resources might be thus utilized. Casework, which could still be brief, would come to an end once this plan had been put into effect. Task-centered casework is a means of alleviating certain problems for which clients request help. If the agency has the resources to alleviate these problems in a straightforward manner by meeting the client's request, then casework intervention may not be needed. Casework should be utilized with those clients who need expert help in designing and effecting courses of action to remedy their difficulties.

ACUTE SITUATIONAL PROBLEMS

Some problems of living brought to the attention of caseworkers are of very short duration, lasting from a few days to a week or two. These are generally problems involving some critical situation in the life of an individual or family. They require immediate action since delay is often intolerable. Hence, a resolution even if a poor one, is usually effected rather quickly. A family whose dwelling has burned down or who arrives in a strange community without funds, a man whose wife has been hospitalized leaving him with the care of small children, a runaway adolescent, a disoriented traveler at a terminal, are all examples of potential clients who may present problems of this type to social agencies. In fact, some agencies, notably Traveler's Aid Societies, deal largely with acute, situational problems.

Casework treatment is normally limited to the duration of the problem. Few cases last more than three interviews, which may well be as it should be, since by that time the client, with the help of the caseworker (or without), has usually made some accommodation to his problem.

Caseworkers are likely to regard such termination as "premature," however, since there are usually ramifications of the immediate problem, or other problems, that "should" be dealt with. Some practitioners in fact, seem to hold the view that the provision of help for a temporary difficulty ought to be a vestibule for gaining entrance into the client's inner world of problems, where much good can be done. If a client has been able to work out a transitory problem, so this theory goes, he may gain the confidence necessary to grapple with "basic" issues in his life. These beliefs bear little relation to what clients seem to want from caseworkers. To the extent that practitioners hold them, however, they are less likely to be of help to clients whose goals are bounded by the emergencies of the present moment.

The present model, with some adaptations, may provide a useful framework for the treatment of problems of this type. Suppose a father requests a plan for care of his children because his wife has just died and he must immediately return to work. Furthermore, he says, he needs a child care plan by the day after tomorrow or otherwise he will lose his job. Thoroughly indoctrinated as we are with knowledge about grief and mourning, our first inclination may be to explore the expected depression in the father and in the children. His need to return at once to work may be interpreted, in fact, as an evasion of the necessary psychological tasks of mourning. The temptation to classify this problem as reactive emotional distress is great. If this is done, one has set the stage to explore and work through a depression. However, such fathers have a marked proclivity to stick to their priorities, which are to obtain child care first and then to manage their mourning, with or without help. One brings also to such a case concerns about "permanent planning" for the children. However, permanent planning for children probably has no more meaning than permanent planning for adults.

By classifying this father's problem as inadequate resources, in the same way that the father classified it, it might be possible to guide him in obtaining an array of services that would tide him over the immediate crisis. Let us suppose that the father is prepared to assume the task of procuring the needed resources with the caseworker's help. By acquainting him with available day care, homemaker service, and temporary foster home resources and discussing their pros and cons, the caseworker enables the father to make knowledgeable choices; or other alternatives may be recommended such as using relatives and friends for child care.

Obviously, the steps of the model need to be compressed, with perhaps a definition of the problem, formulation of the task and beginning work on it taking place within the first interview. The task itself, might be completed within a few days in many cases. Although the time and interview limits of the model would not generally apply, the client should be given an estimate of the time it might take to work out some resolution of the problem. The typical once-a-week schedule of hourly interviews may need to be radically modified. In some cases daily interviews may be required; in other situations (such as sometimes occur at Traveler's Aid), a client may spend the better part of a day in a collaborative effort to resolve a problem.

PRACTITIONERS IN AUTHORITATIVE ROLES

In a number of settings, caseworkers may be required to intervene to protect children against abusive or neglectful parents, or to take action on the behalf of clients who cannot act for themselves (such as individuals with acute mental illness), or to serve certain societal interests (in the case of juvenile or adult offenders). In such situations, the caseworker may be confronted with a reluctant "client" who has not asked for his "services."

Although he may attempt to secure the client's cooperation, the caseworker may need to take certain actions regardless of what the client thinks of them. He may have an abusive parent taken to court, may recommend that an overtly psychotic person be committed, or have an offender's parole revoked. That authoritative, unilateral actions *may* be taken in such situations sets protective casework apart from other kinds of practice. Does the present model have any applicability to practice situations in which caseworkers have authoritative roles?

It does, we think, if we can make a distinction between functions of the caseworker in these situations. His "protective" functions can perhaps be distinguished from his functions as an expert who may help the client solve certain problems. In some cases, these functions may be congruent; for example, a youthful offender may want the caseworker to help him stay out of trouble, but in others they may diverge: a parent may deny he has abused his child, despite overwhelming medical evidence to the contrary, and reject the caseworker's attempts at intervention. The second kind of case obviously presents the greater difficulty.

In normal application of the model we suggest termination if the caseworker cannot uncover a problem that a client expressly wants help with. Matters are not so simple when the caseworker must try to stick with the situation, even though the client wants no further part of him. Perhaps the key is that the caseworker need not operate under the pretense that he is there "to help" the client, after it is clear that the client does not want his help.

We suggest that in such cases the caseworker make quite explicit at the beginning the distinction between his protective and helping functions. He may offer to help the client work out possible problems that are contributing to the difficulties that have precipitated the agency's intervention. A time-limited "problem search" might be offered. During this process, the caseworker would make as plain as possible his candid evaluation of the client's situation, including the possible consequences the client might be facing. The client then would be given a clear choice: to act or not act on his problem.

Certain target problems might be located through this search: the client's difficulties with whatever formal organizations might be breathing down his neck; inadequacies in his role performance; or problems of social transition, as in the case of abusing or neglectful parents who decide to place their children. Task-centered treatment could be addressed to such problems. Its brevity would fit well with the limited motivation for change characteristic of the reluctant client. If the caseworker were obligated to continue a long-term relationship with the client, then the therapeutic segment of the relationship could be followed by continued supervision or whatever else might be required to meet the protective mandate of the agency.

The client would have the right, of course, to refuse the caseworker's help. He should understand that the caseworker, or someone else, might need to take certain actions regardless of his wishes. And we should understand that such actions, while perhaps necessary, do not constitute casework treatment.

CHAPTER ELEVEN

DEVELOPMENT THROUGH RESEARCH

THE USE OF research as a means of improving practice is an imperative of the present system. We cannot in good conscience recommend the use of our model without the concomitant recommendation that its operations and outcomes be systematically studied. Only through such continuing investigation can we replace convictions with evidence, and begin to fill out the many open spaces within our system of treatment.

We are advocating that research activity be carried on as a relatively standard component of a service program. By this we mean that an agency should set aside part of its budget and a portion of staff time to such activity on a continuing basis. Obviously most facilities do not have the resources to mount large-scale or highly rigorous research undertakings, but even very modest allocations for research would represent a step forward, a step in many cases from a complete standstill.

Research can be conducted in many ways and at many levels. A model of the kind we have developed needs to be tested through experimental designs against other treatment models and against natural processes of change to determine the extent and nature of its contribution to problem alleviation. Such studies need to be combined with intensive investigations of the communication processes between practitioner and client (and between the practitioner and others) in order to increase our understanding of these processes and to ascertain their immediate and long-range effects on the client's problems. Changes in problem states need to be studied over time —apart from, during, and after courses of task-centered treatment. Such research efforts, which are costly and time-consuming and which require specialized research skills, may need to be conducted in special settings. There are other research strategies, however, which can be carried out in settings with minimal research budgets and limited access to research expertness. While these strategies cannot be expected to yield the kind of precise, elaborate findings emanating from more extensive and systematic studies, they have the advantage of producing results that can be applied immediately to the improvement of practice at hand.

In this chapter we will review the research we have conducted thus far in our efforts to develop and perfect the present model. The review will serve three purposes: to communicate the results we have obtained; to identify problems in the model that require further work; and to illustrate kinds of research strategies and methods that can be used in development of the model.

This review will cover the three investigations that comprise the bulk of our empirical work to this point. The first and third, which are quite modest in scope, will be dealt with briefly; the second, a more extensive undertaking, will be considered in some detail. These studies do not include less formal trials of the model conducted in hospital, mental health, family, and child welfare settings.

THE THREE STUDIES—
OBJECTIVES, QUESTIONS, AND SETTING

Since the three studies shared similar goals and questions and were conducted in the same setting, these aspects will be considered in common. The main purpose of these investigations was to contribute to the development of the model. Our intent was not to specify the characteristics of the model in operation or to test its effects in any rigorous way. Rather we were interested in securing data that could be used as a basis for making informed judgments about how the model might be improved. It is a purpose that rests upon our value assumption that systematic, albeit imperfect, data offer a better basis for such judgments than other sources of information.

Perhaps the central guiding question was: What is the fit between the model and the realities of practice? From this question a number of sub-questions were derived: How well are directives of the model carried out? Where they were not, why not? What contingencies not taken into account in the model arise and how are they handled? What forms do treatment strategies and methods broadly suggested by the model assume in the details of practice? Do practitioners use any innovative approaches that might be incorporated into the model? What evidence is there that given inputs in the model are achieving desired effects? Provisional answers to such questions have become the major base for model revisions. The model as presented in this book reflects the incorporation of many of the results of these studies, and certain of the results, as we shall show, have revealed difficulties which will need to be taken into account in further work on the model.

The studies were conducted in a university hospital. The first two were carried out in the Medical Social Service Department, staffed largely by graduate social workers. This department provides casework services to both in-patients and out-patients for a range of psychosocial problems associated with physical illness. The third study was set in an out-patient facility of the Department of Psychiatry which offers psychotherapy, casework, and diagnostic services to adults with predominately psychological and interpersonal problems.

THE FIRST STUDY—
PRELIMINARY TRIALS

The first study was an attempt to secure preliminary data on the operations of the model. It will be discussed primarily as an illustration of how research can be used in the beginning phase of model development. The sample consisted of eight cases referred to the Medical Social Service Department. The clients referred were largely female and of lower income status with a range of illness-related problems similar to those of clients in the second study. The cases were carried by students nearing the end of their first year of graduate social work training at the School of Social Service Administration. The students were supervised by one of the authors (Epstein). Sources of data consisted of specially prepared case recordings and brief, largely self-administered questionnaires completed by eleven clients (some cases involved more than one client.)

The outcomes were generally encouraging: five of the eleven clients reported that the problems they particularly wanted help with were no longer present or had been greatly relieved; four said their problems had been relieved to some extent; the remaining two clients (both adolescents in a case in which the mother was the principal patient) indicated that there had been no problems they had particularly wanted help with. Our main interest at this point, however, was to determine how well different components of the model seemed to work and to identify those components that needed modifications or further development.

While most clients identified the same focus of treatment as did their caseworkers, there were marked discrepancies in some cases. In several cases it proved difficult to help the client formulate a task. The main reason seemed to lie in the complex and multifaceted nature of the problems in these cases, which in varying combinations contained medicosocial, psychological, familial, and economic problems. In at least two cases the initial treatment focus could not be maintained because of the emergence of urgent problems which consumed the attention of both caseworker and client.

One requirement of the model in its preliminary form, that the caseworker's role is to facilitate the client's own problem-solving action, could not be met, strictly speaking, in cases where the client was literally "flat on his back." The recording revealed that the caseworkers engaged in considerable activity —in some cases critical to the outcome of the case—with individuals other than the client (doctors, nurses, relatives, social workers from other agencies, and the like). While such activities had a place in our model, this side of casework practice had been given short shrift.

The model was then revised in the light of these findings. More stress was placed on working through a clear understanding of the task with the client; procedures were developed for handling cases with multiple problems and cases in which work on the task had to be interrupted by emerging crises. The notion of the caseworker as the client's agent in task performance was introduced for the client physically unable to act on his own behalf. The caseworker's activities outside the interview were given greater emphasis. For the most part, these modifications consisted of either the specification of methods of dealing with certain contingencies or the delineation of caseworker activities in what had been "open" areas in the model. In these ways the results of the study were used to create a better differentiated and more fully developed model.

THE SECOND AND MAJOR STUDY

The revised model was then given a second series of clinical trials, also carried out in the Medical Social Service Department. Although it involves a small number of cases, this study represents our most intensive and comprehensive effort to date to apply the model and to examine its operations. It is also offered, as are the other studies presented in this chapter, as a demonstration of the kind of model-developing research that can be carried out with modest resources.

THE PRACTITIONERS. The caseworkers in the second study were twenty social work students in the first-year graduate program of the School of Social Service Administration. Each student practitioner carried one project case as a part of a practicum in the Medical Social Service Department.

The use of students as practitioners in clinical research projects is a well-established practice in the fields of psychiatry and psychology but is somewhat unusual in the field of social work. A few words on this point may therefore be in order, particularly since we used students who were just beginning graduate training.

First of all, most of these students had some prior experience in social work. Nine had from one to six years of social work experience, largely in casework; an additional six had worked in social work capacities one or more summers while undergraduates; only five students lacked any social work experience. If our model were designed for use only by caseworkers with graduate training, the prior experience of our student practitioners would have less bearing, but our intent has been to develop a treatment approach that can be used by caseworkers at the Bachelor's level as well.

In this light our students—college graduates for the most part experienced in social work—probably approximate a typical group of "BA social workers" in respect to qualifications for casework practice. The students were perhaps younger and less experienced than most social workers without graduate training (although such social workers tend to be relatively young and inexperienced). On the other hand, our students had the advantage of very small caseloads, and the benefit of intensive individual and group supervision from both the professional social work staff in the Medical Social Service Department and from the faculty members directing the project. In addition a series of class sessions were devoted to the treatment system as a whole.

While the students lacked the technical skill of highly experienced or professionally trained caseworkers, they did offer a compensatory advantage of particular importance in a project of this kind. They did not come equipped with entrenched theoretical convictions or practice styles that would make it difficult, if not impossible, for them to follow the guidelines of the model.

SELECTION AND REFERRAL PROCEDURES. Since we wished to try out the model on as broad a range of cases as possible, we set forth no special criteria for the selection of project cases. We simply designated the first case assigned to the caseworker as his project case. The project caseload then consisted of an unselected group of cases referred to the Medical Social Service Department as a part of the normal flow of referrals to that Department. The cases were referred largely by hospital physicians or nurses; the referrals were made without knowledge that they were to become project cases.

RESEARCH METHOD. Three major sources of data were utilized in the project: 1) A semistructured interview was conducted with the client immediately after the client's second interview with the project caseworker. The interviewer, an experienced graduate caseworker (Joan Kwiatkowski), elicited the client's perception of the problems that brought him to Social Service, his understanding of time limits of service, his conception of his tasks, his assessment of various aspects of service as far as it had gone, and his expectations of the remainder of service. 2) A second semistructured interview was conducted soon after the last service contact. This interview covered the client's conception of the problems and tasks that had been worked on, what he thought had been accomplished, and again asked him to assess various aspects of service. The project caseworkers were used as the research interviewers, with each caseworker interviewing one client (not the one he treated). 3) In addition to securing biographical data on the clients, the caseworkers recorded each service interview according to a standard outline which specified points to be covered, such as a statement of the initial task formulated by the client and caseworker, problems encountered in task formulation and in maintaining focus on the task, and major interventions used to further the client's task achievement.

CHARACTERISTICS OF CLIENTS REFERRED. Generally individual patients (as opposed to families) were referred to project caseworkers or in some cases sought their services. While in several cases other family members also became clients (as will be specified later) in most cases the individual referred received the bulk of the caseworker's attention.

The clients referred ranged in age from fourteen to eighty-one; a fifth were adolescents (nineteen and under); a fifth older persons (sixty and over); and about half fell between the ages of forty and fifty-nine. About a third were currently married; a fourth were widowed, and another fourth, single. At point of referral, the sample was divided evenly between in-patients and out-patients. An almost equal division occurred along racial lines (eleven clients were black and nine white). All but five were women.

The project clientele was fundamentally working class, with all but two clients falling in categories IV and V in the Hollingshead (1957) Two-Factor Index. Only two clients had received more than a high-school education, although it should be noted that four of the clients referred were adolescents still in school. Seven of the twenty clients were receiving public assistance.

TARGET PROBLEMS. Since our typology of target problems was still being formulated when the project began, it was not given as much attention as were other aspects of the model in the training of the students. As a result, clear statements of the target problem were lacking in many of the cases. Moreover, in some cases it was found that the client presented possible tasks at the very beginning, often in the form of requesting the caseworker's help in carrying through some course of action, such as securing financial assistance. In fact, in the initial research interview, about a third of the clients expressed their problems essentially in these terms. In these cases, exploration of the problem tended to occur in the process of task formulations, rather than as a preceding step. It was clear that the problem typology was not being uniformly used to guide the caseworker to a task.

It was possible, however, to use the caseworker's recording as a basis for determining his perception of the major target problem in each case. The following distribution of problems was obtained:

MAJOR TARGET PROBLEM	NUMBER OF CASES
Interpersonal conflict	1
Dissatisfaction in social relations	3
Relations with formal organizations	1
Social transition	4
Role performance	3
Reactive emotional distress	2
Inadequate resources	6
Total	20

The problems were connected with physical illness or disability in one manner or another: for example, insufficient resources to meet the costs of illness; problems of transition from hospital to home; difficulties in caring for an ill family member; special vocational needs resulting from disability; and emotional reactions to sickness or impending surgery. The client's definition of the major target problem was obtained from the initial research interview. When the client's and worker's statements were compared, it was found that there was substantial agreement in nine cases; in ten cases, there was agreement in some respects, disagreement in others—for example the caseworker and client might agree on the general problem area but might have differing views on the specific focus of the difficulty; in only one case (in which the client denied she had any problem) was there complete disagreement. The degree of agreement between client and worker was also measured on a five-point scale. According to this measure, sixteen cases fell at points 4 or 5 (indicating a reasonable level of agreement); the remaining four fell at point 2, interpretable as a low level of agreement. On the whole then, the findings suggest that practitioners, in conformity with the model, were proceeding from a base of accord with the client on the nature of the major problem.

Qualitative analyses of the caseworkers' and clients' statements about the problem led to several revisions of the model that have already been incorporated and presented. Examples include the notion of the two levels of problem expression on the client's part and procedures for ranking problems with the client in order of their importance to him.

Other results of this analysis may serve as the base for future revisions. One such finding concerns various departures from the model in respect to initial problem exploration and clarification. We noted earlier that in some cases, preliminary formulation of the task *preceded* exploration of the problem, with the latter carried out in connection with discussion of the task. In other cases, the steps involving determination of the target problem were compressed into a few minutes of the initial interview, particularly when the problem appeared to be fairly clear-cut. While such flexibility and telescoping may be useful, the caseworker in some cases may have moved too readily to task formulation, without sufficient examination of the problem. In any event, we need to take into account the contingencies presented when the client seeks help to implement a task he is already working on or when the problem, as stated by the client, appears to require little exploration or analysis.

While the first study gave us a basis for developing better guidelines for handling cases in which new problems arise during the course of treatment, the present study suggests that still more work is needed in this area. Cases characterized by an assortment of shifting problems posed considerable difficulty for the model. In the case of Miss L, for example, one finds an adolescent girl with problems involving her depression over her illness, her relationship with her boy friend and parents, her adjustment to school, and her plans after leaving the hospital. In typical adolescent fashion, her concerns shifted from one problem area to another, sometimes within the space of a few minutes. Although the eventual focus was on her problems of social transition, a good deal of attention was paid to other problems, often leading the caseworker into the kind of drifting conversation we seek to avoid. This kind of case raises some hard questions: How much focusing on specific problems is possible or desirable? Under what conditions does responsiveness to the client's concerns of the moment take precedence over the need to be systematic? What special contingencies should be developed for this kind of client? Is the model really appropriate in cases of this sort? Partial answers to such questions have been developed in earlier chapters. More complete and satisfactory answers will require further thought and further research.

As expected we experienced some difficulties with the problem classification scheme itself. The categories could be readily applied in cases in which isolated or clearly diverse problems occurred. Thus in the case of Miss M, whose fears of impending surgery were followed by dilemmas about her post-hospital plans, it was clear that the problems were those of reactive emotional distress and social transition. Difficulties in using the scheme were most pronounced in cases in which more than one category might apply to a complex problem situation.

For example, Mrs. S was upset about her elderly mother's dependence on her. According to Mrs. S, her mother expected her to "do everything for her." Various problem categories were possible: reactive emotional distress, interpersonal conflict, or role performance. The choice in this case was important since it would influence the focus of the caseworker's efforts. The category decided upon—role performance—was based in part on how Mrs. S viewed the problem situation and how the situation might be best dealt with. She did not appear to see the primary change target as her emotional distress about the situation, and it did not seem feasible to work with both mother and daughter to bring about reciprocal change in their behavior as would need to be done if the problem were interpersonal conflict. Thus the target problem was cast in terms of her performance in her role as daughter—and her task became what she might do to help her mother become more independent. A good deal of uncertainty surrounded these choices. Another caseworker (or another caseworker-supervisor combination) might have decided differently. Such uncertainties, or sources of unreliability, are perhaps necessary costs in a scheme that attempts to take into account both how the client views a problem situation and what can be done about it.

The problem categories were too broad to guide treatment planning in any precise way. It may be of some use to know that Mrs. S has a problem of role performance, but we also want to know what kind of role performance problem this is. A related piece of research (Wingard, 1971) demonstrated this point on a larger scale. The problem classification was applied to 138 cases in a combined family-service/mental-health facility. While it was possible to classify 87 percent of the problems through use of the system—46 percent of them fell into the interpersonal conflict category and 30 percent were classified as problems of role performance. Clearly the system needs to be better articulated—that is, the general groupings need to be broken down into smaller classifications.

Despite its limitations the typology did help to identify major problems and to direct task formulation in many cases. In most, we think, it enabled the practitioner to organize his efforts to explore and analyze the clients' concerns.

THE AMOUNT AND DURATION OF SERVICE. In only one case (Mrs. N), in which fifteen client interviews were held, did the number of interviews exceed the limit of twelve suggested in the model. The median number of interviews was six. All cases (of the nineteen in which tasks were formulated) received at least three; six cases received at least eight interviews. In most cases there were face-to-face contacts with individuals other than the client, principally doctors and relatives. There was considerable telephone communication, particularly with social agencies in efforts to locate resources and to implement the client's use of them. The time span of service was measured from the first to the last client interview. No case exceeded the four-month limit of the model, although five cases reached the limit. The median time period was two months, with seven cases not exceeding a month in duration.

In respect to number of client interviews and duration, most project cases fell toward the lower rather than the upper limits of the model. The reason probably lies in the limited life span of most of the target problems, which were typically related to illness or hospitalization of brief duration.

Service tended to be more concentrated than it would be in usual practice, however. In a third of the cases, for example, clients were seen more often than once a week; and we must also keep in mind the considerable amount of activity with non-clients, a feature of practice that is unfortunately not taken into account in gauging service limits in brief treatment models, ours included.

The model calls for the caseworker and client to work out an agreement on the approximate duration and amount of service in the first two interviews. According to the caseworkers' recordings of these interviews, agreements were reached with eleven clients but only eight of these clients (when seen after the second interview) could recall such an agreement having been made. In some cases the client, naturally with a good deal on his mind in these interviews, may not have "heard" or understood the caseworker's reference to the limits of service. In others, the discussion of such limits may have been less conclusive than the caseworker's recording indicated. By the third or fourth interview such agreements had been reached, in most cases, according to the caseworker's recording, and all but two clients in the final research interview were able to recall that limits had been set on the amount and duration of service. In some cases these limits were revised as service proceeded.

It is clear that the caseworkers got off to a slow start in the setting of service limits and that they were not always successful in getting across their intentions to clients. The practitioner's misgivings about limiting service seemed to be a factor in some instances, as often seems to be the case in the practice of planned short-term treatment. With some clients there was understandable reluctance to set service limits prior to clarification of the problem and tasks. These cases were usually those in which the initial steps of the model took more than the expected amount of time to accomplish. In still others there was legitimate question about setting arbitrary limits for closed tasks that seemed naturally self-limiting—such as securing a certain kind of financial assistance. The later observation in fact was instrumental in developing different guidelines for setting service limits for open as opposed to closed tasks (chapter 5).

One problem emerged that we have only partially taken into account in refinement of the model up to this point. In several cases a greater amount of service was contracted for than seemed needed. When treatment was focused on a closed task which was completed early, termination was a natural step. It was more difficult to know what to do when the case was centered on an open task which appeared to be carried about as far as it could be prior to the agreed-upon terminal point. In general, we need to build in more flexibility into the lower limits of our treatment model—eight interviews or two months of service may be too much in some cases. Practitioners and designers of short-term approaches are accustomed to thinking of difficulties in respect to the upper limits of service. Whether or not we are providing clients with enough treatment, has been our major preoccupation. That our short-term treatment design may really be too long-term for some clients needs to be taken into account and its ramifications thought through.

TASK FORMULATION. We attempted to determine what client tasks were formulated in each case. Statements of tasks were first identified in the caseworkers' recordings. These were then checked against the clients' responses as reported by the research interviewers, since a task by definition must be agreed upon by both the caseworker and client. Through this process we were able to identify a total of twenty-nine tasks stated both by the caseworker and the client, although we did not require the statements to be expressed in the same form or similar in every detail.

The case records and research protocols were read by three readers, one of whom was the faculty supervisor. Tasks included in the final listing were those identified by at least two of the readers (and in most instances by all three). This listing is presented in Table 1, along with outcome data which will be considered shortly. The statements are "abstracts" of the caseworkers' own task formulations.

As can be seen, tasks were formulated and worked on in all but one of the twenty cases referred to the project. The one case in which no task emerged (Mrs. I) was completed in two interviews after a problem search revealed no difficulties the client expressly wished help for. The remaining cases were di-

vided about equally between those in which work was organized around a single task (nine) and those in which multiple
tasks were formulated (ten). Multiple-task cases were generally confined to two tasks worked on concurrently. Sub-tasks,
while used, were not sufficiently well formulated to permit systematic analysis.

In all but four of these nineteen cases, at least one of the
identified tasks was formulated during the first or second interviews in keeping with guidelines of the model; in all cases
but one a task was formulated by the end of the third interview. In most cases the initial formulation of the task was not
altered greatly, although in several the initial task was altered
because of the emergence of new problems or changes in the
clients' circumstances or condition. With few exceptions clients
appeared to have a reasonable conception of the treatment
focus, judging from their statements in the initial research interview, although there seemed to be considerable variation in
the clients' notions of who was responsible for carrying out
the task. In some cases the client formulated the task along
lines suggested by the model; in others he viewed the caseworker as being responsible for carrying out the course of action agreed upon, and in still others the client's conception of
who was responsible was not clear.

The content of the major tasks reflected the range of the
target problems. No single type of task dominated. Most fell
into the following general categories: securing financial assistance for illness or disability (seven); taking action to help a
family member with a medicosocial or behavior problem
(five); securing regular or home employment or vocational
training (four); planning for care of family member (four);
planning for own discharge (three); other tasks involved work-

Table 1

CLIENT TASKS AND DEGREE OF ACHIEVEMENT

Clients*	Tasks	Degree of Achievement
Mrs. A	To resolve feelings of distress about being a burden on daughter.	Substantial
	To secure financial assistance for medical expenses.	Complete
Mrs. B	To secure homemaker for care following surgery.	Complete
Mrs. C and Mr. C	To find work or useful activity.	Substantial
Mr. D	To find home-bound employment.	Complete
Mrs. E	To secure larger allowance from department of welfare.	Minimal
	To plan for mentally retarded daughter.	Partial
Mr. F	To secure disability benefits.	Minimal
	To contact vocational rehabilitation agency.	Minimal
Mrs. G	To work out plan for paying medical bills.	Complete
Mr. H	To secure a job.	Partial
Mrs. I	No task formulated	
Mrs. J	To work out plan for mentally retarded child.	Substantial
Mr. K and Mrs. K	To secure social security benefits.	Partial
	To secure home-bound employment.	Minimal
Miss L	To develop plan for post-discharge living arrangements and work.	Substantial
	To alleviate fears of surgery.	Substantial
Miss M	To plan post-discharge care.	Substantial
Mrs. N	To make decision about additional surgery for handicapped child.	Complete
	To provide adequate home care for the child.	Substantial

Mrs. O	To work out placement plan for son.	Partial
Mrs. P	To plan for pregnant daughter's medical care, living arrangements, and school.	Partial
	To help mentally retarded son get along better at school.	Substantial
Mrs. Q	To help son overcome bedwetting.	Complete
	To secure better housing.	Minimal
Miss R, Mr. R and Mrs. R	To secure information about financial assistance for medical payments.	Partial
Mrs. S	To help her mother to be less dependent.	Partial
	To help her husband lose weight.	Partial
Miss T	To help boy friend establish relationship with their illegitimate child.	Partial
	To secure psychiatric help for emotional problems.	Complete

* The client originally referred is listed first, followed by other family members seen as clients.

ing through of emotional distress associated with illness or obtaining a specific resource, such as housing or a homemaker. Closed tasks (seventeen) were more frequent than open tasks (twelve); most of the former were concerned with obtaining specific kinds of financial assistance, employment or other resources.*

THE CASEWORKER'S ACTIVITIES IN RELATION TO THE TASK. Our primary source of data on the caseworker's inputs was his own recording, which unfortunately did not yield as detailed a picture of his activities as we had hoped for. We could only occasionally tape interviews. Thus we were not able to obtain the kind of "process" data that would have enabled us to test our notions about responsive and systematic communication or to study closely the caseworker's specific contribution to the client's task achievement. We did obtain, however, a general picture of the caseworker's activities from the recording and from our supervisory conferences with the caseworkers. Some of these impressions have already found expression elsewhere in this book, particularly in chapter 7.

In general, the focus of the caseworker's activities was on the client's task, as the model prescribed. It is fair to say that the bulk of the caseworker's communication after the initial interview was task-related. More than in usual practice, explicit structuring operations were used to keep the client focused on the task, though in many cases these did not prove necessary after the caseworker and client became "locked-in"

---

* Findings reviewed in preceding sections are presented in greater detail in Joan Kwiatkowski, *Task-Centered Casework: A Study of the Initial Phase* (School of Social Service Administration, University of Chicago, doctoral dissertation in progress).

on a specific area of work. The caseworker's initiation of discussion of the task and reporting on his own task-related activities outside the interview at the beginning of interviews proved useful ways of maintaining focus.

It is difficult to generalize about the caseworker's use of change-oriented methods given our rather limited data base. Our impression is that greater use was made of direction and encouragement than would be so in usual practice. These techniques were often used to stimulate the client to try out task-related behaviors in respect to care of others, finding work, or securing resources.

Efforts to enhance the client's awareness were limited largely to his awareness of others and his situation, including his understanding of family members in his care, of job possibilities, of medical procedures and his own physical condition, and of potential resources. Enhancement of a client's self-understanding was used in a number of cases, however, for example: to help a client understand emotional aspects of his distress over his illness, to help him clarify needs and goals in relation to post-discharge plans or resources to be secured, or to help him understand the consequences of his behavior in relation to the care of others. In most cases, enhancing awareness and direction were used with relatives, physicians, nurses, and representatives of organizations to present a picture of the client's characteristics and needs and to secure services on his behalf.

In the great majority of cases these interventions were concentrated on the tasks, in keeping with the basic strategy of the model. A fair amount of caseworker activity was not related to agreed-upon tasks, however. In certain cases a good deal of caseworker effort was spent in exploring or dealing with other problems, sometimes present from the beginning, sometimes arising during the course of treatment. In evaluating such activities we concluded that some, while not particularly fruitful, were perhaps inevitable if the caseworker was to be appropriately sensitive to changes in the client's life situation and to the emergence of new problems requiring new tasks.

Other activities could be called providing "incidental services," such as communicating requests to medical staff, which usually required little time but provided clients with needed kinds of help. Allowances should certainly be made for extension of this kind of assistance. While the worker's efforts in many of these cases might have been more task-related, we came away with the thought that the model at its present state of development should require only that the bulk of the practitioner's activities be task-centered. Until further trials have been constructed and more knowledge accumulated, provision should be made for a certain amount of "free play" in the model.

TASK ACCOMPLISHMENT. The principal measure of outcome for this model is the extent to which a given task is accomplished, since the efforts of caseworker and client are concentrated on task achievement. Generally a measure of task accomplishment is also a measure of the degree of alleviation of the specific problem to which the task is addressed. While there may be some exceptions to that rule, assessment of problem reduction used in the initial study was found to yield results almost identical to a measure of task achievement.

Progress on each task was rated according to the following scale:

TASK ACHIEVEMENT SCALE

Points

4 COMPLETELY ACHIEVED.

This rating applies most clearly to closed tasks that are fully accomplished, e.g., a job has been found, a homemaker secured, financial assistance obtained. It may also be used for open tasks that are fully accomplished "for all practical purposes"; if a couple's task was to reduce quarreling a rating of (4) could be given if they reached a point where hostile interchanges occurred infrequently, no longer presented a problem, and they saw no need for further work on the task.

3 SUBSTANTIALLY ACHIEVED.

The task is largely accomplished although further action may need to be taken before full accomplishment is realized. Thus if the task is to improve work performance, significant improvement would merit a rating of (3) even though further improvement would be possible and desirable.

2 PARTIALLY ACHIEVED.

Demonstrable progress has been made on the task but considerable work remains to be done. For example, if the task is to obtain a job, a rating of (2) could be given if the client has been actively looking for work and found a job he could (and might) take but was reluctant to. Or this rating would be appropriate for a couple who had made some head-

way on a shared task of finding things of mutual interest to do together even though they and the caseworker may be dissatisfied with their progress.
Specific evidence of task accomplishment is required however. A rating of (2) should not be given
just on the basis of positive motivation, good intentions, or expenditure of effort.

1 MINIMALLY ACHIEVED (OR NOT ACHIEVED).
This rating is used for tasks on which no progress
has been made or on which progress has been insig-
nificant or uncertain. If a client's task were to locate and enter a suitable vocational training program, a rating of (1) would be given if the client
were unable to locate a program, even though much
effort had gone into searching for one.

This scale was applied to the list of twenty-nine tasks that had
been identified in the project caseload. Three sets of independent ratings were obtained for each task. Judgments were
based both on the caseworker's recording and the client's responses to the research interviews. On all but two of the tasks,
the judgments were either in perfect agreement (twelve) or two
of the three were in accord (fifteen). Disagreements were generally one point apart on the scale. The final outcome ratings
in Table 1 represent unanimous or majority opinion; in the
two instances in which no agreement at all was reached, the
middle rating was used as the final one. Given the relatively
high level of agreement among the judges, the final ratings
may be regarded as a reasonably reliable measure of task accomplishment. Judges were also asked to designate tasks as
"open" or "closed." The reliability for this measure was also

satisfactory, with nineteen of the twenty-nine sets of three judgments in perfect accord.

The ratings presented in Table 1 give a fairly specific picture of "movement" in the various cases. Since the outcome measure is applied to tasks, one can pinpoint where progress has occurred. More important, measurement is concentrated on an assessment of the focal efforts of the caseworker and client on what they set out to do.

In these respects, the Task Achievement Scale has certain advantages over more conventional global measures of changes that are based on the assumption that certain treatment goals apply to all cases. Such measures often fail to give specific information on precisely what changes have occurred. Thus we may rate clients such as Mrs. B as having experienced some improvement in her material circumstances, but this rating gives us only a vague notion of how things are better for her. The picture becomes clearer when we say that she secured financial assistance for medical expenses. It is also possible that this accomplishment, which she regarded as quite important, might not even have been detected in a gross measure of change in her material circumstances. Measures based on the assumption that certain changes are to be expected in all cases may be irrelevant, if not misleading. For example, changes in functioning or family interaction, which are typical of across-the-board measures in casework research, might have been germane in certain of our cases but not in others.

Assessment of task achievement has at least one important drawback as a measure of outcome: variation in tasks makes it difficult to make comparisons across cases. Thus Mrs. E's task of working out a plan for her mentally retarded daughter is of a far greater order of difficulty than Miss T's task of securing psychiatric help. Of course much the same problem exists, though it is often not recognized, in standard measures, which can take on diverse meanings according to the case. In assessment of task achievement, however, the problem seems an inevitable part of the measurement strategy. An eventual solution may lie in developing ways of classifying tasks according to type or degree of difficulty, so that similarities and differences can be taken into better account. Until such a solution can be devised, it may be advisable to list the tasks, together with their ratings, as we have done, so that the reader can make his own judgments about task variations.

Table 2

DEGREE OF ACHIEVEMENT BY TYPE OF TASK

| Achievement | Client Tasks | | Total |
	Open	Closed	
Complete	1	7	8
Substantial	7	—	7
Partial	4	5	9
Minimal	—	5	5
Total	12	17	29

Table 2 presents one attempt to relate achievement to a classification of tasks. As will be recalled, tasks were categorized as being either open (lacking a natural terminal point) or closed, that is, capable of being fully achieved. As can be seen, task accomplishment varied according to whether the task was open or closed.

Ratings for open tasks tended to cluster in the two middle categories (substantial and partial achievement), while ratings for closed tasks tended to fall in the extreme categories (complete or minimal achievement). This pattern of variation results in part from the way in which tasks and levels of accomplishment were defined since, by definition, open tasks are difficult to achieve completely but closed tasks can be. Nonetheless, the findings demonstrate the importance of taking into account the "open-closed" dichotomy in evaluating results obtained from application of the Task Achievement Scale.

Moreover the difference in results were not entirely forced by the nature of our definitions. It was encouraging to learn that some demonstrable progress was made on all open tasks and that well over a third of the closed tasks were completely achieved. On the other hand, the lack of any appreciable progress on five closed tasks is a matter of concern. That about half the tasks were no more than partially achieved suggests there is considerable room for improvement in the model.

It is also possible to use the Task Achievement Scale to derive a measure of case progress, either through combining the ratings for different tasks or using the rating for one task as an index. Using the latter approach, we classified cases according to the highest level of task achievement occurring in each. It was found that at least one task was completely or substantially achieved in eleven cases and partially achieved in six; there were only two cases in which no demonstrable progress was made on any task.

CHANGES IN THE CLIENT'S OVERALL SITUATION. Another measure of outcome was based on the client's gross evaluation of changes in his overall situation from the point of his first contact with the caseworker to the closing research interview. Global measures of change of this type are not viewed as central to the assessment of task-centered work since the aims of service are relatively specific. Nevertheless such measures are of some use in determining the impact of task accomplishment in the client's life in general. It must be recognized, of course, that factors other than task achievement or service as a whole may contribute to changes in a client's life situation.

Of the nineteen clients, fourteen, or 74 percent, thought that their overall situations were better or much better at the end of service than at the beginning, although one (Mrs. Q) made it clear that service had nothing to do with the change. The remaining five reported that their situations were essentially the same, or in one case "slightly better." When the relation between task achievement and situational change is examined, one finds that of the ten clients who were able to accomplish at least one task completely or substantially, nine reported their situations had improved. By contrast, of the eight clients who were not able to complete one task more than partially, five reported that their situations were essentially the same or, in one case (Mrs. Q), that change was not related to service.* Thus it appears that the level of task achievement is related to the client's view of change in his overall situation, which suggests (though does not prove) that task achievement in these cases had a beneficial effect on the client's general condition and circumstances. In any event, it seems clear that successful work on the task was part of a general pattern of positive change.

It was noted earlier that outcomes reported for brief time-limited treatment tend to equal or surpass the improvement rate that seems to be the norm for long-term, open-ended treatment. The results of the present study conform to this

* The differences are statistically significant at $p < .05$ Fisher's Exact Test.

generalization. If the Task Assessment Scale is used as a measure, then seventeen of twenty cases, or 85 percent of the cases, showed some improvement. (The one early terminator is included in these calculations since drop-outs are normally included in determining overall improvement rates.) If we use a grosser estimate—the client's assessment of change in his overall situation—then fourteen of twenty cases, or 70 percent, show improvement. (We are counting Mrs. Q as improved for this purpose since clients' opinions about the relation of change to treatment are normally not included in assessments of outcome; on the other hand, we are not counting as improved one client who reported her situation as only slightly better.) Even though our treatment approach is not aimed at promoting overall "improvement," the comparative findings suggest that our clients did reasonably well in respect to this criterion.

PROBLEMS REMAINING. One criticism made of short-term treatment models is that they do not allow for sufficient time to attend to all the problems the client may want help with. Accordingly we asked clients in the closing research interview if they had any personal or family problems for which they wished help. The great majority (fourteen) said they did not, four indicated they did, and in one case a response was not elicited. Of the four who expressed a need for further help, three (Mrs. E, Mr. F, and Mrs. Q) were clients whose task achievement was either minimal or partial and who thought that further help of some kind (not necessarily from the project caseworker) might be of some use in accomplishing their goals. The fourth (Mrs. P) was a client whose tasks were carried out successfully but who perceived continuing problems with her emotionally disturbed, mentally retarded son. She planned to continue her contacts with one of the hospital clinics.

It is clear that most clients at the end of service did not perceive problems *they wanted help with,* although rest assured these clients, like most of us, were beset with problems of one kind or another. But they thought—and some clients expressed this spontaneously—that they could deal with them on their own. The three clients who were not successful in carrying out their tasks and who wanted further help cannot be ignored, however. In all three cases it was decided that the caseworker and client had gone as far as they could with the tasks, within the time allotted. Moreover, further extension of the service period (which was in fact made in one of the cases) was not seen as a solution. In all three cases further help, at least for the incomplete tasks, needed to come from organizations which controlled certain services and resources the clients wanted.

THE CLIENT'S ASSESSMENT OF SERVICE. The client's opinion of the service he has received can contribute in at least two ways to model development: 1) when objective criteria of treatment effectiveness are lacking, the client's evaluation of his treatment experience provides a basis for shaping the treatment design; 2) even if it is not used to guide the selection of treatment input, information on the client's reaction can at least give us an idea of what to expect when given approaches are used. In the closing research interview, the client was presented with a series of statements describing or pertaining to particular components of the model and was asked to indicate whether he agreed or disagreed with each statement. The results are given in Table 3.

Table 3

CLIENT'S ASSESSMENT OF SELECTED ASPECTS OF SERVICE

Item	Statement	Number of Clients	
		Agreeing	Disagreeing
1.	I received the kind of help I wanted from Social Service.	17	1 *
2.	My caseworker came through with the kind of help he (she) said he was going to give me when we started.	19	0
3.	I liked the idea of deciding at the beginning how long casework service was going to last.	14	3 *
4.	Casework service lasted about the right length of time.	17	2
5.	Casework service was a little too brief; I could have used a few more more sessions.	2	17
6.	Casework service was far too brief; it should have continued for much longer period of time.	1	18
7.	I was confused a lot of the time about what my caseworker was trying to do	3	16
8.	My caseworker concentrated too much on me; he should have tried to do more to change the attitude of others or to get me services that I needed.	4	15
9.	There were a lot of things on my mind which we did not have time to discuss.	3	16
10.	My caseworker should have given me more advice about what to do.	1	18
11.	My caseworker gave me too much advice about what to do.	0	19
12.	My caseworker seemed to have a lot of confidence that I would be able to work out my problems	17	2
13.	In my last discussion with my caseworker, I got some good ideas about what I might do about problems I still have.	16	2 *

* Totals are less than 19 because responses of "uncertain" or "not applicable" were excluded.

It is clear that the clients' evaluation of these various aspects of service was uniformly quite positive—indeed, to the extent that one suspects a definite "halo effect" was operating. From these and other data there is little doubt that most clients had a generally favorable reaction to service. Their responses to particular items may have been influenced by an overall positive set. Still, more than half the clients made at least one negative response, indicating some effort to respond to the statements in a discriminating way.

With few exceptions, clients thought that service was relevant to their needs and that the caseworker delivered the kind of help promised. Obviously, the brief duration of service and the early planning of termination (items 3 through 6) troubled few clients; in fact, these aspects of service were generally endorsed. The client who had the greatest objection to the brevity of service was Mr. D, a seventeen-year-old boy with a cardiac condition who had successfully completed his task and who had an otherwise positive reaction to service. But apparently he wanted to continue to see his caseworker. He was the one client who thought service was far too brief even though he could express no further problems he wished to work on.

Responses to items relating to the worker's treatment operations (items 7 through 12) suggest that the client found the caseworker's efforts understandable, did not regard the treatment focus as excessively restrictive or inappropriate, indicated that the amount of direction provided by the caseworker was neither inadequate nor excessive, and thought the caseworker was generally encouraging. Item 8 is of interest since the number of clients responding negatively was higher than for any other item in this series. Two of these clients were rather disturbed individuals: one was overtly delusional during one of the treatment interviews and the other was highly eccentric and probably schizophrenic. They may have reacted with some sensitivity to the caseworker's probing of their feelings and behavior, even though there was no evidence in the recording that this was done to any great extent.

Responses to the final statement suggest that the caseworker's attention in the final interview to what the client might do about remaining problems met with a favorable response, although the item itself is rather vague. At least we have from it an indication that the clients came away with an understanding of what the caseworker attempted to accomplish in the last session.

In the initial research interview, the client had completed a comparable set of items which were worded to elicit his assessment of the same aspects of service as he had experienced them up to that point. A comparison of the client's initial and terminal responses was carried out to determine the direction and degree of change in the client's evaluation of service components over the course of treatment.

Of the items presented in Table 3, eight were selected for this comparison (1, 2, and 7 through 12). The items on time limits and duration (3 through 6) were not included since, as noted, these matters had not been discussed with several clients during the initial interviews, and the last item was dropped since it contained no parallel in the first administration.

One point was given for each response that reflected a positive evaluation of a service aspect. Since there were eight items, scores could range from zero (no positive response) to a maximum of eight (all responses positive). A response of "uncertain" was counted as a lack of a positive response. As was seen in Table 3, the clients' response to this set of items on the second administration were generally positive; they tended to be somewhat less positive on the first administration, though all but two clients give positive responses to the majority of the eight items.

Initial and terminal scores were compared for each client with the following results: nine clients had higher scores in the second administration; eight had the same scores each time, and the scores of two clients declined. The changes were statistically significant ($p < .05$, Wilcoxon Signed Ranks Tests). Two items, 2 and 8, were the major contributors to this generally positive shift. In the first research interview, several clients were either uncertain or doubtful that the worker was coming through with the kind of help he had said he would give, and several thought that too much time was being spent trying to help them understand what they were doing wrong. Such reservations were expressed less frequently in the last research interview.

If a model is working well, one would expect that a client's satisfaction with it would increase as treatment begins to "pay off." Although a definitive explanation for the shift in the scores is not possible, it does seem as if the positive change in the client's reaction was related to certain sequential operations of the model, namely movement from exploring the client's role in his difficulties to helping him do something about them. The change in the clients' responses, although not of great magnitude, also suggests that clients were not responding with blanket approval of everything the caseworker did. If so, there would have been no systematic difference between the two sets of scores.

A final set of items was addressed to the client's evaluation of service as a whole (as opposed to particular aspects of service). Since the clients' responses showed little variation across these items, the results of only one will be reported. This item asked for the clients' overall assessment of the helpfulness of service on a five-point scale. Eighteen clients responded with the two top ratings of the scale: "I could not have gotten along without the service," and "I was considerably benefited." The remaining client (Mrs. Q) thought she was "neither helped nor harmed," the fourth point of the scale. The third point "I was slightly benefited" and the lowest rating "I would have been better off without Social Service contact" were not used by the clients.

Although these ratings were generally congruent with the clients' positive evaluation of discrete aspects of service, they still seemed suspiciously high. In particular it was puzzling that of the eight clients whose task achievement at best was partial, seven should have rated service as "helped substantially" or "could not have gotten along without it." Since clients had completed a comparable item on the first research interview, the earlier ratings were examined to see what light they might shed. The initial ratings were high enough to rule out the possibility that the final ratings had been massively inflated by interviewer biases or other factors in the second research interview. At the first administration, ten of the seventeen clients who completed the item thought that they were being considerably benefited by treatment or they would not be able to get along without it. On the other hand, six thought that service was giving them only slight benefit, and one could not yet see any positive results. Thus there was some positive shift in the ratings between the two points of time, as one would expect if the model was operating as it should and if the ratings were responsive to its operations.

Even so it is difficult to interpret ratings given by clients

such as Mr. F, Mr. and Mrs. K, and Mrs. O, who rated service as being maximally helpful at both points of time but
who achieved only minimal or partial accomplishment of their
goals. Possibly these clients, as well as some others, were reacting in part to the helping *efforts* expended by an interested
and concerned caseworker, a factor that may also have influenced the clients' evaluations of particular aspects of service.
These efforts may have been particularly valued by clients
whose dependence on others may have been heightened by
physical illness and whose need for human warmth was accen-
tuated by an impersonal hospital environment.

Even if we grant that the clients' reactions may have been
inflated by their appreciation of a caseworker's efforts, or simply his attention, it is reasonable to assume that this evaluation on the whole reflected their belief that service was actually helpful. Although we cannot attribute these positive
evaluations to particular characteristics of the caseworkers' inputs, we can say that the model, as a whole, was well received
by the clients.

This same item on helpfulness of service was used in three
other studies of casework, all conducted in a family agency
(Kogan, 1957, p. 118; Shyne, 1960, pp. 175–76; Reid and
Shyne, 1969, p. 117). Some comparative findings may be of
interest. If we include the rating of the client (Mrs. I), who
terminated at the end of the second interview and who did not
rate service as helpful, we find that eighteen of the twenty
clients, or 90 percent, reported that they had benefited considerably from service or could not have gotten along without
it. In the other studies in which clients responded to the same
item we find that the percentages of clients who rated the
helpfulness of service at these levels ranged from 16 to 54 per-

cent for various sub-groups. In the present study, 10 percent of the clients rated service as having no positive effect. In the other studies, percentages for ratings at this level ranged from 7 to 50. The middle rating (service was slightly beneficial), which was not used by clients in our study, was given by a fifth to half of the clients in the comparison studies. We have suggested some reasons why clients might have perceived our service as particularly helpful; these reasons may help explain why ratings on this item surpass those in other studies, none of which dealt with a population of hospital patients. Moreover, casework services in the other studies were more likely to be addressed to more intractable problems—disturbances in family relations, for example. Nevertheless, one cannot help but be encouraged by these comparative data. At least they suggest that we may be on the right track in developing a casework approach that clients regard as particularly helpful.

THE THIRD STUDY: TASK-CENTERED CASEWORK IN A PSYCHIATRIC CLINIC

The third project involved six cases carried by three experienced, graduate caseworkers in a psychiatric outpatient facility in the university hospital. We were particularly interested in testing the model with trained caseworkers, since our previous trials had been largely with students, and in applying it to the kinds of problems treated by a mental health facility, the base of much casework practice.

These cases were followed in biweekly meetings of the caseworkers and the authors. The meetings served purposes both of training the caseworkers in use of the model and providing the authors with detailed data on the cases. In addition, the caseworkers provided the authors with their case recordings and completed on each case an instrument which requested data on the nature of the problems and the tasks, the major interventions used, and task accomplishment.

In general, the project demonstrated the applicability of the model to the kind of clientele served by the clinic. Although the caseworkers selected cases at intake for the trials of the model, they had little difficulty locating cases or in applying the model once a case had been selected. In all cases, target problems were identified, service limits were set, and tasks were formulated and worked on.

In four cases at least one task was substantially achieved, and in the remaining two at least one task was partially achieved, according to collective judgments based on available data. It might be noted that each caseworker originally agreed to apply the model to one case—that they decided on their own initiative to then apply it to a second case is some indication that they perceived value in this approach.

As with the first two studies, various things learned from this project have been incorporated into the model in its present form; one of the cases (Mr. Todd) has been previously used for illustrative purposes. Some additional observations are worth sharing, however.

First, the identification of target problems was a more difficult and time-consuming undertaking than it had been in our medical social service cases. The problems presented by the clients were certainly more pervasive and complex: a student with a mixture of anxieties and conflicts about academic performance, social relationships, and career choice; a woman with stomach cramps and a recent weight loss which she attributed to disturbances in her relationship with her boy friend; a young wife whose depression over her husband's threat to leave her had precipitated a suicide attempt; a young man who had "no will to do anything" because his fiancée had broken off with him but refused to tell him why; a middle-aged man who felt he was "stumbling along socially and professionally"; and finally Mr. Todd whose work and social problems have already been detailed.

One anticipated difficulty—locating target problems within the scope of the model—did not emerge as the clients themselves seemed mostly concerned with problems in their interpersonal relations, role performance, or in making choices about future roles. Still it often proved difficult to determine the *exact* target problem or problems. In most cases, more than one problem was dealt with, with shifts in emphasis as treatment proceeded. The problem typology proved to be of greater use than had been expected (judging from our previous studies) in locating and defining areas of concern. Because the practitioners possessed more knowledge of human behavior and had more clinical training, the problem formulations were more fully developed with more elaborate statements of possible psychological and social causes.

The tasks were open in all cases but one; in most cases two concurrent, related tasks were pursued. As a rule, a good deal of effort was spent in attempting to clarify the task, with tasks undergoing reformulations in most cases. Thus, in one case, the client's task was first put in terms of his trying to resolve his feelings of loss over his broken engagement; but when it became clear that he still had hopes of winning his ex-fiancée back, his task was reformulated in approximately the following terms: to resolve his feelings about his relationship with his girl friend either through getting her back or giving her up.

In another case emphasis shifted from one concurrent task—enhancing academic performance—to the other—making a decision about career goals. In general, efforts to clarify and reformulate tasks were closely related to, and were sometimes a product of, the worker's efforts to help the client effect change. Thus in the last example, analysis of the client's difficulties in applying himself to a particular kind of course work revealed uncertainties about his interest in the work, which in turn led to a reexamination of his career goals. Changes of tasks in these cases seemed to be a function of shifts in the clients' perceptions and motivations rather than a function of changes in the clients' situations as was more characteristic of the medical service cases.

Service limits were set and adhered to in all cases. The number of interviews in three cases, reflecting the agreed-upon limits, ranged from six to fourteen, with four of the cases having ten or more sessions. As in the medical service cases, it was often difficult for the caseworker and client to agree on a precise number of interviews, as the model suggests, within the first two interviews. The persistence of this difficulty has led us to the provisional suggestion that the caseworker at least inform the client in the first interview about the probable maximum length of treatment, with the understanding that a more precise estimate will be arrived at as soon as feasible. This possibility, of course, will need to be tested out. That these cases required more interviews than the medical service cases was probably due in part to the greater complexity of the problems and tasks and in part to the fact that two of the three caseworkers were not used to working under brief treatment conditions. It is interesting to note that one of these two workers, who expressed misgivings that a thirteen-interview contract originally agreed upon might not be sufficient, finally concluded that a shorter contract would actually have been desirable to avoid certain "transference problems" that arose toward the end of the case.

Virtually all of the caseworkers' treatment activities were carried out through individual interviews with the client. The caseworkers' treatment approaches tended to be psychoanalytically oriented, with various incorporations of other points of view. They were able to adapt their basic approaches to the present model without noticeable strain.

Perhaps the principal technical issue concerned the scope and depth of a caseworker's efforts to help a client work through obstacles to task achievement. It was expected that much of the caseworkers' efforts in the kind of problems encountered in these cases would be devoted to helping the clients identify, understand, and work through obstacles to task accomplishment. And this proved to be generally true. But there is much to be learned about how such obstacles can best be resolved. An obstacle may have roots in certain difficulties which are in turn connected to other difficulties. As a result the caseworkers often found themselves in labyrinths of interconnected problems, with the danger of losing their focus on the task.

Thus the young woman with physical complaints revealed herself to be a lonely, dependent person who was tied to an unhappy affair with an abusive man because she "had no place to go." It was decided her task would be to establish other relationships that could provide her with needed emotional support and gratification. One obstacle was her need to cling to her boy friend. Her dependency on him seemed to be a carry-over of her extreme dependency on her mother, who had died some years before but whom she still mourned.

A good deal of attention was given to the client's still unresolved feelings about her mother's death, which led to a consideration of the client's earlier relationship with her. The caseworker managed to relate these themes back to the task by helping her see the connection between her need for her mother and her boy friend. There was general uncertainty, however, about whether she had gone too far or not far enough. The client did make progress on the task, as she was able to turn more to her sisters and to achieve a greater degree of independence from her boy friend. But we cannot say if more might have been accomplished had the caseworker concentrated more on immediate obstacles or had gone even further in the direction she pursued.

A related issue concerned handling transference reactions, that is, the tendency of the client to attribute to the practitioner characteristics of others, particularly important figures in his earlier life. Consideration of such reactions in full could easily take the client far afield from the task. This issue was handled in two cases by focusing on those aspects of the transference that could be related to the task. For example, in the case of the young wife whose upset over her husband's divorce threat precipitated a suicide attempt, the problem she wanted most to work on was her tendency to be self-effacing and submissive in relations with others, including her husband. Her task was to "learn how to make appropriate demands on others." Her difficulty in so doing seemed connected to her lack of trust in people, which was manifested in her relationship with the caseworker. This aspect of her feelings toward the caseworker was dealt with, through interpretations, while other possible aspects of the transference were left alone. This selective use of the transference seemed to offer a way of resolving the issue, although it may not be adequate with clients whose transference reactions are stronger or more pervasive.

FROM PAST TO FUTURE

The three studies served their essential purpose of providing data that could be used to further the development of the task-centered model. We could not help but be encouraged by the progress achieved by most of the clients studied, even though we have no way of specifying how much of their progress was due to our interventions. Perhaps the results assume greater significance when they are viewed as supported by a sizable body of evidence that attests to the relative effectiveness and efficiency of brief, time-limited approaches.

Our research has raised questions about our methods that will require further thought and work to answer. That was its function. The picture of the model-in-action (as portrayed by our data) is of course less clean-cut and definitive than the picture of the model-in-the-abstract, as set forth in the earlier portion of the book. This is as it should be. In fact, the effort to reconcile disparities between such pictures—by bringing practice realities into greater alignment with the directives of the treatment design, and vice-versa—is the essence of model development.

Our initial purpose was to develop a system of casework that would prove useful to practitioners, teachers, and students of casework. We think we have accomplished that goal and hope that others share our conviction. While we recommend our approach for immediate use, we also recommend that every effort be made to improve upon it. Regardless of the form of casework we choose to practice, we must at the same time work with what we have and try to make it better.

Our own progress will depend largely upon our ability to pursue model-building research and upon our willingness to be guided by its results. The temptation to transform tentative ideas into ultimate truths is hard to resist. Self-fulfilling prophecies are more comfortable than predictions that must be continually exposed to empirical testing. The choice is between the certainty of unchallenged belief and the uncertainty bred by scientific endeavor. It is the latter choice we must make and stick to if the promise of our system of casework is to be fully realized.

REFERENCES

Abrams, S. T. et al. 1966. "The Caseworker's Activity in Joint Interviews." Unpublished group Master's thesis, Graduate School of Social Work, New York University.

Aldrich, C. K. 1968. "Community Psychiatry's Impact on Casework and Psychotherapy." In *Smith College Studies in Social Work* 38:102–15.

Avnet, H. H. 1965. "How Effective is Short-Term Therapy." In *Short Term Psychotherapy*, ed. Lewis R. Wolberg. New York: Grune and Stratton.

Bartlett, H. M. 1970. *The Common Base of Social Work Practice*. New York: National Association of Social Workers.

Bellak, L. and L. Small. 1965. *Emergency Psychotherapy and Brief Psychotherapy*. New York: Grune and Stratton.

Bergin, A. E. 1971. "The Evaluation of Therapeutic Outcomes." In *Handbook of Psychotherapy and Behavior Change: An Empirical Analysis*, eds. A. E. Bergin and S. L. Garfield. New York: Wiley.

Blenkner, M., J. Jahn, and E. Wasser. 1964. *Serving the Aging: An Experiment in Social Work and Public Health Nursing*. New York: Community Service Society.

Briar, S. 1971. "Family Services and Casework." In *Research in the Social Services: A Five-Year Review*, pp. 108–29. New York: National Association of Social Workers.

Briar, S. and H. Miller. 1971. *Problems and Issues in Social Casework*. New York: Columbia University Press, 1971.

Brieland, D. 1968. "Use of Teams in Child Welfare—Background and Perspectives." In *Differential Use of Manpower: A Team Model for Foster Care*, pp. 1–10. New York: Child Welfare League of America.

Carkhuff, R. R. and M. Alexik. 1967. "Effect of Client Depth of Self-Exploration Upon High and Low Functioning." *Journal of Counseling Psychology* 14:350–55.

Carroll, E. J., M.D. 1964. "Family Therapy, Some Observations and Comparisons." *Family Process* 3:178–85.

Davis, I. P. 1971. "The Caseworker's Use of Influence in Counseling Parents." Doctoral dissertation (in progress), School of Social Service Administration, University of Chicago.

Dubin, R. 1969. *Theory Building*. New York: Free Press.

Ehrenkranz, S. M. 1967a. "A Study of Joint Interviewing in the Treatment of Marital Problems: Part I." *Social Casework* 48:498–502.

——1967b. "A Study of Joint Interviewing in the Treatment of Marital Problems." *Social Casework* 48:570–74.

Eiduson, B. T. 1968. "Retreat from Help." *American Journal of Orthopsychiatry* 38:910–21.

Eisenberg, L. and E. M. Gruenberg. 1961. "The Current Status of Secondary Prevention in Child Psychiatry." *American Journal of Orthopsychiatry* 31:355–67.

Epstein, L. 1962. "Differential Use of Staff: A Method to Expand Social Services." *Social Work* 4:66–72.

——1965. "Casework Process in Crisis Abatement." *Child Welfare* 44:551–55.

Eysenck, H. J. 1966. *The Effects of Psychotherapy*. New York: International Science Press.

Family Service Association of America. 1969. *Facts and Trends on FSAA Member Agencies: 1969*. New York: Department of Systems and Statistics, FSAA.

Ford, D. H. and H. B. Urban. 1963. *Systems of Psychotherapy: A Comparative Study*. New York: Wiley.

Fowler, I. A. 1967. "Family Agency Characteristics and Client Continuance." *Social Casework* 48:271–77.

Friel, T., D. Kratochvil, and R. R. Carkhuff. 1968. "Effect of Client Depth of Self-Exploration on Therapists Categorized by Level of Experience and Type of Training." Unpublished manuscript, State University of New York at Buffalo.

Gambrill, E. D., E. J. Thomas, and R. D. Carter. 1971. "Procedure for Sociobehavioral Practice in Open Settings." *Social Work* 16:51–62.

Garfield, S. L. 1971. "Research on Client Variables in Psychotherapy." In *Handbook of Psychotherapy and Behavior Change: An Empirical Analysis,* eds. A. E. Bergin and S. L. Garfield, pp. 271–99. New York: Wiley.

Garfield, S. L. and M. Wolpin. 1963. "Expectations Regarding Psychotherapy." *Journal of Nervous and Mental Disease* 137:353–62.

Geist, J. and N. M. Gerber. 1960. "Joint Interviewing: A Treatment Technique with Marital Partners." *Social Casework* 41:76–83.

Gilbert, A. 1960. "An Experiment in Brief Treatment of Parents." *Social Work* 5:91–97.

Goldstein, A. P., K. Heller, and L. B. Sechrest. 1966. *Psychotherapy and the Psychology of Behavior Change.* New York:

Gottlieb, W. and J. Stanley. 1967. "Mutual Goals and Goal Setting in Casework." *Social Casework* 48:471–78.

Gottshalk, L. A., P. Meyerson, and A. A. Gottlief. 1967. "Prediction and Evaluation of Outcome in an Emergency Brief Psychotherapy Clinic." *Journal of Nervous and Mental Disease* 144:77–95.

Haley, J. and L. Hoffman. 1967. *Techniques of Family Therapy.* New York: Basic Books.

Hamilton, G. 1951. *Theory and Practice of Social Casework.* 2d ed. New York: Columbia University Press.

Hare, M. K. 1966. "Shortened Treatment in a Child Guidance Clinic: The Results of 119 Cases." *British Journal of Psychiatry* 112:613–16.

Harper, R. A. 1959. *Psychoanalysis and Psychotherapy.* Englewood Cliffs, N. J.: Prentice-Hall.

Heine, R. and H. Trosman. 1960. "Initial Expectations of the Doctor-Patient Interaction as a Factor in Continuance in Psychotherapy." *Psychiatry* 23:275–78.

Hellenbrand, S. 1961. "Client Value Orientations: Implications for Diagnosis and Treatment." *Social Casework* 42:163–69.

Hoehn-Saric, R. et al. 1964. "Systematic Preparations of Patients for Psychiatry, I: Effects on Therapy Behaviors and Outcomes." *Journal of Psychiatric Research* 2:267–81.

Hollingshead, A. B. 1957. "Two Factor Index of Social Position." Unpublished paper, copyright by author. New Haven, Connecticut.

Hollingshead, A. B. and F. C. Redlich. 1952. *Social Class and Mental Illness.* New York: Wiley.

Hollis, F. 1964. *Casework, a Psychosocial Therapy.* New York: Random House.

——1966. "Development of a Casework Treatment." Final report to the National Institute of Mental Health. New York, Columbia University School of Social Work.

Hollis, F. 1967a. "Explorations in the Development of a Typology of Casework Treatment." *Social Casework* 48:335–41.

——1967b. "The Coding and Applications of a Typology of Casework Treatment." *Social Casework* 48:489–97.

——1968. "Continuance and Discontinuance in Marital Counseling and Some Observations on Joint Interviews." *Social Casework* 49:167–74.

——1970. "The Psychosocial Approach to the Practice of Casework." In *Theories of Social Casework,* eds. R. W. Roberts and R. H. Nee, pp. 33–76. Chicago: University of Chicago Press.

Jackson, D. D. and J. H. Weakland. 1961. "Conjoint Family Therapy: Some Considerations in Theory, Technique, and Results." *Psychiatry* Supplement to 2, May.

Joint Commission on Mental Health Health of Children. 1970. *Crisis in Child Mental Health: Challenge for the 70's.* New York: Harper and Row.

Kaffman, M. 1965. "Short-Term Family Therapy." In *Crisis Intervention: Selected Readings,* ed. H. J. Parad, pp. 202–19. New York: Family Service Association of America.

Kerns, E. 1970. "Planned Short-Term Treatment: A New Service to Adolescents." *Social Casework* 51:340–46.

Kluckhohn, F. 1958. "Variations in the Basic Values of Family Systems." *Social Casework* 39:63–72.

Kogan, L. S. 1957. *A Study of Short-Term Cases at the Community Service Society of New York.* New York: Institute of Welfare Research, Community Service Society.

Krasner, L. 1971. "The Operant Approach in Behavior Therapy." In *Handbook of Psychotherapy and Behavior Change: An Empirical Analysis,* eds. A. E. Bergin and S. L. Garfield, pp. 612–52. New York: Wiley.

Kwiatkowski, J. 1971. "Brief, Task-Centered Casework: A Study of the Initial Phase." Doctoral dissertation, School of Social Service Administration, University of Chicago.

Levitt, E. E. 1963. "The Results of Psychotherapy with Children: A Further Evaluation." *Behavior Research and Therapy* 1:45–51.

Lewis, H. 1971. "Practice Science and Professional Education: Developing a Curriculum Responsive to New Knowledge and Values." Paper read at Symposium on Effectiveness of Social Work Intervention: Implications for Curriculum Change, 14–15 January 1971, at Fordham University, New York, N.Y.

Malan, D. H. 1963. *A Study of Brief Psychotherapy*. Springfield, Ill.: Charles C. Thomas.

Mayer, J. E. and N. Timms. 1970. *The Client Speaks: Working Class Impressions of Casework*. New York: Atherton Press.

McGuire, M. T. 1965a. "The Process of Short-Term Insight Psychotherapy, I." *Journal of Nervous and Mental Diseases* 141:83–94.

——1965b. "The Process of Short-Term Insight Psychotherapy, II: Content, Expectations, Structure." *Journal of Nervous and Mental Diseases* 141:219–30.

Meltzoff, J. and M. Kornreich. 1970. *Research in Psychotherapy*. New York: Atherton Press.

Meyer, C. H. 1970. *Social Work Practice: A Response to the Urban Crisis*. New York: Free Press.

Meyer, H. J., E. F. Borgatta, and W. C. Jones. 1965. *Girls in Vocational High: An Experiment in Social Work Intervention*. New York: Russell Sage Foundation.

Muench, G. A. 1964. "An Investigation of Time-Limited Psychotherapy." *American Psychologist* 19:476. (Abstract of paper given at 1964 annual convention of the American Psychological Association.)

Mullen, E. J. 1968. "Casework Communication." *Social Casework* 49:546–55.

Mullen, E. J., R. M. Chazin, and D. M. Feldstein. 1970. *Preventing Chronic Dependency*. New York: Institute of Welfare Research, Community Service Society of New York.

Murray, E. and W. Smitson. 1963. "Brief Treatment of Parents in a Military Setting." *Social Work* 8:55–61.

National Center for Health Statistics. 1966. *Characteristics of Patients of Selected Types of Medical Specialists and Practitioners: United States July 1963–June 1964*. Washington, D.C.: Public Health Service Publication No. 1000, Series 10, No. 28.

Nebl, N. 1971. "Essential Elements in Short-Term Treatment." *Social Casework* 52:377–81.

Oppenheimer, J. R. 1967. "Use of Crisis Intervention in Casework with the Cancer Patient." *Social Work* 12:44–52.

Parad, H. J. 1963. "Brief Ego-Oriented Casework with Families in Crisis." In *Ego-Oriented Casework: Problems and Perspectives,* eds. H. J. Parad and R. R. Miller, pp. 145–64. New York: Family Service Association of America.

Parad, H. J. and L. G. Parad. 1968a. "A Study of Crisis-Oriented

Planned Short-Term Treatment, Part I." *Social Casework* 49:346–55.

Parad, H. J. and L. G. Parad. 1968b. "A Study of Crisis-Oriented Planned Short-Term Treatment, Part II." *Social Casework* 49:418–26.

Parad, L. G. 1971. "Short-Term Treatment: An Overview of Historical Trends, Issues, and Potentials." *Smith College Studies in Social Work* 41:119–46.

Parry, J. 1967. *The Psychology of Human Communication.* New York: American Elsevier Publishing Co.

Patterson, C. H. 1966. *Theories of Counseling and Psychotherapy.* New York: Harper and Row.

Perlman, H. H. 1957. *Social Casework: A Problem-Solving Process.* Chicago: University of Chicago Press.

——1968. *Persona: Social Role and Responsibility.* Chicago: University of Chicago Press.

——1970. "The Problem-Solving Model in Social Casework." In *Theories of Social Casework,* eds. R. W. Roberts and R. H. Nee, pp. 131–79. Chicago: University of Chicago Press.

Phillips, E. L. and M. S. H. Johnston. 1954. "Theoretical and Clinical Aspects of Short-Term Parent-Child Psychotherapy." *Psychiatry* 17:267–75.

Phillips, E. L. and D. N. Wiener. 1966. *Short-Term Psychotherapy and Structured Behavior Change.* New York: McGraw-Hill.

Pinkus, H. 1968. "A Study of the Use of Casework Treatment as Related to Selected Client and Worker Characteristics." Unpublished doctoral dissertation, Columbia University School of Social Work.

Pins, A. M. 1971. "Changes in Social Work Education and Their Implications for Practice." *Social Work* 16:5–15.

Powers, E., and H. Witmer. 1951. *An Experiment in the Prevention of Juvenile Delinquency.* New York: Columbia University Press.

Rapoport, L. 1970. "Crisis Intervention as a Mode of Brief Treatment." In *Theories of Social Casework,* eds. R. W. Roberts and R. H. Nee, pp. 265–312. Chicago: University of Chicago Press.

Rapoport, R. 1965. "Normal Crises, Family Structure, and Mental Health." In *Crisis Intervention: Selected Readings,* ed. H. J. Parad, pp. 75–87. New York: Family Service Association of America.

Reid, W. J. 1964. "Practitioner and Client Variables Affecting Casework Treatment." *Social Casework* 45:586–92.

——1967. "Characteristics of Casework Intervention." *Welfare in Review* 5:11–19.

———1970. "The Implications of Research for the Goals of Casework." *Smith College Studies in Social Work* 40:140–54.

———1971. "Sectarian Agencies." In *Encyclopedia of Social Work,* 16th ed., Vol. II, eds. R. Morris et al., pp. 1154–63. New York: National Association of Social Workers.

Reid, W. J. and B. L. Shapiro. 1969. "Client Reactions to Advice." *Social Service Review* 43:165–73.

Reid, W. J. and A. Shyne. 1969. *Brief and Extended Casework.* New York: Columbia University Press.

Ripple, L. 1964. *Motivation, Capacity, and Opportunity: Studies in Casework Theory and Practice.* Chicago: School of Social Service Administration, University of Chicago.

Roberts, R. W. and R. H. Nee, eds. 1970. *Theories of Social Casework.* Chicago: University of Chicago Press.

Rosenblatt, A. 1968. "The Practitioner's Use and Evaluation of Research." *Social Work* 13:53–59.

Rosenthal, D. and J. D. Frank. 1958. "The Fate of Psychiatric Clinic Out-Patients Assigned to Psychotherapy." *Journal of Nervous and Mental Diseases* 127:330–43.

Sacks, J. G., P. M. Bradley, and D. F. Beck. 1970. *Clients Progress Within Five Interviews.* New York: Family Service Association of America.

Satir, V. 1964. *Conjoint Family Therapy.* Palo Alto: Science and Behavior Books.

Scherz, F. H. 1970. "Theory and Practice of Family Therapy." In *Theories of Social Casework,* eds. R. W. Roberts and R. H. Nee, pp. 219–64. Chicago: University of Chicago Press.

Schlien, J. M. 1966. "Comparison of Results with Different Forms of Psychotherapy." In *Psychotherapy Research,* eds. G. E. Stollak, B. C. Guerney Jr., and M. Rothberg, pp. 156–62. Chicago: Rand McNally.

Schwartz, E. E. and W. C. Sample. 1966. *First Findings from Midway.* Chicago: School of Social Service Administration, University of Chicago.

Shaw, R., H. Blumenfeld, and R. A. Senf. 1968. "A Short-Term Treatment Program in a Child Guidance Clinic." *Social Work* 13:81–90.

Sherman, S. 1959. "Joint Interviews in Casework Practice." *Social Work* 40:20–28.

Shyne, A. 1960. "Former Clients Evaluate a Youth Service Program." *Children* 7:175–79.

Sifneos, P. E. 1967. "Two Different Kinds of Psychotherapy of Short Duration." *American Journal of Psychiatry* 123:1069–74.

Silverman, P. R. 1970. "A Reexamination of the Intake Procedure." *Social Casework* 51:625–34.

Simon, B. K. 1970. "Social Casework Theory: An Overview." In *Theories of Social Casework,* eds. R. W. Roberts and R. H. Nee, pp. 353–94. Chicago: University of Chicago Press.

Simon, H. A. 1957. *Administrative Behavior.* New York: Macmillan.

Small, L. 1971. *The Briefer Psychotherapies.* New York: Bruner-Mazel.

Smalley, R. E. 1967. *Theory for Social Work Practice.* New York: Columbia University Press.

——1970. "General Characteristics of the Functional Approach: A Brief Statement of the Origins of this Approach." In *Theories of Social Casework,* eds. R. W. Roberts and R. H. Nee, pp. 79–128. Chicago: University of Chicago Press.

Stein, E. H., J. Murdaugh, and J. A. Macleod. 1969. "Brief Psychotherapy of Psychiatric Reactions to Physical Illness." *American Journal of Psychiatry* 125:1040–47.

Strupp, H. H., R. E. Fox, and K. Lessler. 1969. *Patients View Their Psychotherapy.* Baltimore: Johns Hopkins Press.

Stuart, R. B. 1967. "Applications of Behavior Theory to Social Casework." In *The Socio-Behavioral Approach and Applications to Social Work,* ed. E. J. Thomas, pp. 19–33. New York: Council on Social Work Education.

——1970. *Trick or Treatment: How and When Psychotherapy Fails.* Champaign, Ill.: Research Press.

Studt, E. 1968. "Social Work Theory and Implications for the Practice of Methods." *Social Work Education Reporter* 16(2):22–46.

Thomas, E. J. 1970. "Behavioral Modification and Casework." In *Theories of Social Casework,* eds. R. W. Roberts and R. H. Nee, pp. 181–218. Chicago: University of Chicago Press.

Truax, C. B. 1967. "A Scale for the Rating of Accurate Empathy." In *The Therapeutic Relationship and Its Impact,* eds. C. Rogers et al., pp. 555–68. Madison: University of Wisconsin Press.

Truax, C. B. and R. R. Carkhuff. 1967. *Toward Effective Counseling and Psychotherapy: Training and Practice.* Chicago: Aldine.

Truax, C. B. and K. M. Mitchell. 1971. "Research on Certain Therapist Interpersonal Skills in Relation to Process and Outcome." In

Handbook of Psychotherapy and Behavior Change, eds. A. E. Bergin and S. L. Garfield, pp. 299–344. New York: Wiley.

Turner, F. J. 1964. "A Comparison of Procedures in the Treatment of Clients With Two Different Value Orientations." *Social Casework* 45:273–77.

Uhlenhuth, E. H. and D. B. Duncan. 1968. "Subjective Changes with Medical Student Therapists." *Archives of General Psychiatry* 18:428–38.

Urban, H. B. and D. H. Ford. 1971. "Some Historical and Conceptual Perspectives on Psychotherapy and Behavior Change." In *Handbook of Psychotherapy and Behavior Change: An Empirical Analysis,* eds., A. E. Bergin and S. L. Garfield, pp. 3–35. New York: Wiley.

Wallace, D. 1967. "The Chemung County Evaluation of Casework Services to Dependent Multi-Problem Families." *Social Service Review* 41:379–89.

Watzlawick, P. 1967. *Pragmatics of Human Communication.* New York: Norton.

Wingard, G. 1971. "Service Patterns in the Southwest Suburban Family Service and Mental Health Center." Unpublished paper, School of Social Service Administration, University of Chicago.

Wolberg, L. R. 1965. *Short-Term Psychotherapy.* New York: Grune and Stratton.

INDEX